T. V. S. Ramamohan Rao

Economic Efficiency of the Organizational Decisions of the Firm

With 53 Figures

Springer-Verlag Berlin Heidelberg New York
London Paris Tokyo Hong Kong

Professor Dr. T. V. S. Ramamohan Rao
Indian Institute of Technology
Kanpur, U. P. 208016, India

ISBN 3-540-51570-4 Springer-Verlag Berlin Heidelberg New York Tokyo
ISBN 0-387-51570-4 Springer-Verlag New York Berlin Heidelberg Tokyo

Printing: Weihert-Druck GmbH, Darmstadt
Bookbinding: T. Gansert GmbH, Weinheim-Sulzbach
2142/7130-543210

PREFACE

Over the past several years there has been an awareness that markets, contractual arrangements, and hierarchical organizations can be utilized as alternative modes of coordinating resource utilization in the context of the firm. In most practical situations mixed forms of organization are more frequent. That is, non-market coordination mechanisms are being utilized even in predominantly market oriented economies.

The reasons for the use of one of these organizational modes over the others are still being examined extensively. Very often, asset specificity and bilateral monopoly, risk sharing under uncertainty, transaction cost considerations, and/or technological externalities (economies of scope) have been considered as the major reasons for preferring one of these modes over the others. However, the ultimate effect on the performance of the firm, of any of these aspects which result in the adoption of any specific organizational pattern, has to be through the cost curve and/or the demand curve.

The neoclassical welfare concepts, which have been developed to examine the efficiency in the functioning of markets, are well known. The sources of inefficiency in the performance of the firm under different market structures are also well documented. However, there is as yet no well established set of concepts to examine the economic efficiency of the other organizational forms. It is not clear that the neoclassical welfare concepts are not relevant even under the new organizational setting. Studies of this nature are a relatively new area of economic research.

The neoclassical theory of the firm proceeds with welfare analysis in three steps:

(a) details the choice sets available to the principals and agents involved in exchange within the organizational echelons of the firm as well as on the market,

(b) examines the motivations and objectives of the consumers of the products of the firm and managers within the organization, and

(c) specifies the equilibrating mechanisms to resolve possible conflicts.

The implications of each of these for the costs and demand curves of the firm form the basis on which welfare concepts have been developed.

As of now a similar analytical structure to examine the welfare effects of mixed organizational forms is not available. Even the relationship between an optimal choice of organizational design and the external market conditions is generally not clear. Only a few attempts at identifying the information flows within the organization and across firms in a market are available.

To return to the realm of the theory of the firm and examine the efficiency of mixed modes would perhaps be more concrete and analytically tractable if an identification of certain generic types of internal decisions can be attempted. Such an analytical process can clarify issues relating to the

(a) role of internal decisions on the structure and conduct of firms,

(b) role of the market on the design of the internal organization, and

(c) relative contribution of the organizational and market modes towards the efficiency of firms.

New conceptual developments along these lines are warranted.

The basic purpose of the present work is to approach this problem by taking into account the aggregate quantitative decisions generally presented in the balance sheet and profit and loss account of a firm. Such an approach has the prospect of being amenable to empirical testing in a more concrete form than what has been possible so far.

This somewhat ambitious excursion into the conceptual domain was enthusiastically supported by the Indian Council of Social Science Research, New Delhi. I am grateful to the ICSSR for the financial assistance which they provided. However, the views expressed here are entirely those of the author and the ICSSR is in no way responsible for the contents.

Parts of this work have been presented at various seminars. Many of the comments and suggestions which I received helped me in rethinking about specific issues. Several chapters of this work were also published in international and Indian journals. I appreciate the encouragement so received. Some friends alerted me to new estimation problems that arise in the context of such studies. I could take advantage to these possibilities and develop some new results. A few of these have already been published. But they should perhaps form the basis for another monograph.

On the whole, the welfare economics of organizational decisions appears to be a fertile ground for much needed research in economic theory as well as applied econometrics.

T.V.S. Ramamohan Rao

Kanpur

August 1988

TABLE OF CONTENTS

CHAPTER 1

THE FIRM AND ITS ORGANIZATION

1.1. MARKET EXCHANGE

Consider the economy of Robinson Crusoe. This one person organization is such that Crusoe

(a) owns all the resources utilized in production,

(b) has full control on the use of resources, and

(c) receives the entire produce for own use.

Similarly, it is obvious that Crusoe

(a) has perfect information regarding consumption requirements,

(b) the information is effortlessly and costlessly available to organize production,

(c) there are no rival demands from any others, and

(d) there are no rival producers who will cater to consumption requirements.

Further, the primitive production process is such that

(a) the costs of production and consumption (or sale) are identical,

(b) all the costs attributable to production and consumption are private as well as social costs, and

(c) the costs are unique, and trivially the minimum possible, since there is no rival organizational mechanism for production.

Under these conditions Crusoe can easily calculate the effort vs. consumption requirements in arriving at an optimal utilization of the available resources. Stated in terms of the conventional diagrams of the theory of the firm it follows that

(a) the demand curve for output is fixed and Crusoe has perfect information about it,

(b) the cost curves are fully known, and

(c) Crusoe will be fully motivated to maximize the net gain from his effort since the returns accrue to him exclusively.

As a result the effort he puts in and the costs of production are the minimum necessary for a given level of output.

Largeness of the economy in terms of the number of individuals, variety of needs, and variagated means of production create changes in the production requirements. With such complexity the need for organization and coordination arises. The first principle of economic analysis is of course the division of labor and the associated efficiency of production. Perforce this sets up the need for exchange. Consequently there will be a need to redefine and reassess the efficiency of different organizational forms that are available.

In contrast to the Crusoe economy certain fundamental changes have been brought about by the process of specialization and division of labor. In particular,

(a) the motiviations of individual consumers which generate the demand for goods are distinct from those which motivate the same or other individuals to organize production and supply goods for exchange,

(b) the agencies which provide resources to the firm can be distinct from the organizers of production,

(c) the motivations of the managers of production can be distinct from those of the consumers, and

(d) there are innumerable exchange mechanisms which might operate.

In such a milieu it would be necessary to set up mechanisms

(a) to elicit information about the demand curve which depends on the consumer preferences as well as the information regarding rival firms in the market,

(b) to identify the sources of supply of resources and set up exchange mechanisms,

(c) to examine the motivations of the various individuals in exchange, and

(d) to identify and implement the organization of exchange.

The market, as an impersonal exchange mechanism, was expected to fulfil all these roles. Hence, the theory of the firm started analysis with some fundamental assumptions.

(a) Every firm in the market can and does possess unambiguous and perfect information regarding the demand curve for its product,

(b) since every one of the rival firms have perfect information about all other firms and their actions none of them can influence the demand curves of other firms through their own actions,

(c) the markets for inputs are such that the output producer has perfect information about alternatives,

(d) being a one person owner-manager organization the firm may not value personal effort explicitly. The costs are only those of the purchased inputs,

(e) if the firm is a one person organization there will be no need to explicitly consider the interpersonal communication and management process within the firm,

(f) the managers of production know the technology of production, or the input output relations perfectly,

(g) production of different firms is unrelated in the sense that the cost curve of any one of them is independent of those of the others,

(h) all transactions are conducted costlessly through the market mechanism, and

(i) all the agents in the exchange process maximize net gains to themselves. In particular, in the interest of maximizing their own profit the managers are induced to choose an input combination which minimizes the cost of producing a given level of output.

1.2. MONOPOLISTIC COMPETITION

The more recent developments of the theory of the firm have, in one way or the other, their origins in the theory of monopolistic competition. Conventionally such market forms are characterized by the existence of a large number of firms selling related or differentiated products.

It is a rather common observation that every product on the market is a collection of various service qualities or characteristics. Most of the consumer goods are also such that there is significant heterogenity of consumer preferences for different service characteristics. In such markets the firm may feel that competition along the price dimension, which is typical in the neoclassical theory of the firm, may not be the best alternative in its quest for obtaining the maximum profits. Instead, non-price competition along some quality dimension may provide relative monopoly power and effective shelter from competition.

One of the major aspects considered in the literature is the concept of the product as a variable. That is, by appropriately choosing a bundle of service characteristics the firm can create an unique quality of the product. These product differences may be genuine from a technological viewpoint or may merely be such as to appeal to the consumer. On some occasions, even the warranty for a product or the reliability of after sales service may prove to be decisive in determining product quality. In yet other cases, like passenger services on an airline, the flight schedules may significantly influence the consumer.

The product choice of the consumer may be affected by yet other characteristics. If the firm produces a wide range of substitutable products with the same plant and machinery it may have a better chance of attracting a wide variety of consumers than it would if it produced only one of them. A similar argument applies in the context of complementary products as well. Similarly, a firm which has a larger inventory stock may be considered to be a more reliable supplier. A similar situation arises even when the firm has access to fairly wide distribution outlets.

Monopolistic competition represents another distinct dimension when viewed as a market form. There are many rival firms in the market and this makes it difficult for any one firm to have complete and cost free information about the behavioral choices of the rival firms. Under these conditions the firm has several choices. The first alternative is to incur search costs to obtain information about the reactions of the rivals which critically affect its own demand curve. However, for any one firm in this market, the information and search costs may be so prohibitive as to prevent it from making attempts to fully resolve endogenous randomness. Essentially the alternative consists in actively choosing a level of demand which the firm wishes to maintain for itself and utilizing advertising and other sales promotion policies to stabilize the market demand curve and smooth production and sales by appropriate inventory policies. These two aspects of demand management also generate internal decisions.

The third alternative reaction from firms in monopolistic competition would be to choose appropriate behavioral modes as an effective reaction to the endogenous randomness. In general, the neoclassical theory of the firm considered the output choice as the only major behavioral mode available to the firm. But, under monopolistic conditions with random demands the firm may choose to fix output and/or price depending on the relative significance of the fixed and variable costs on its cost structure. Price fixation poses new problems for welfare economics.

Further, under this behavioral alternative the firm can no longer be viewed as a profit maximizer. Among the diverse behavioral choices it is possible to find both risk averse and risk taking behavior. Even this aspect of the specification of the motiviations of the firm in its decision making requires a reconsideration of the efficiency concepts and the sources of inefficiency.

On the whole, the theory of monopolistic competition highlights

(a) internal decisions being generated from the necessity to stabilize and/or alter the demand curve of the firm, and

(b) the possibility of the firm pursuing objectives other than profit maximization.

This section and the previous one therefore highlight the possibility of the firm internalizing various decisions affecting the demand side as well as the production process. The motivational aspects being different from profit maximization in such a milieu cannot be ruled out.

1.3. CONTRACTUAL RELATIONS

Before the invention of money, which served as a necessary simplification to the introduction of the market mode of organization the primitive economies had a system of barter exchange of a bilateral or multilateral nature. It served the useful function of enabling specialization and increase in productivity. However, the introduction of money did not eliminate the usefulness of contracting within smaller groups.

The market mode may be particularly suitable if the transactions are recurrent or continuous over time and if there is no information barrier. On the other hand, certain transactions, such as those involving machinery, are infrequent. Under such conditions the buyer may be able to reduce costs in a bilateral exchange instead of incurring wide ranging search costs on the market. Similarly, the purchase of inputs as well as sales on the market may necessitate extensive investments in specific assets in the form of a purchasing or a marketing department. If a specific long term contract can be set up then it may be far more economical to organize the same transactions. It was further pointed out that in imperfect markets the desire on the part of the firm to reduce uncertainty may also induce the management to enter into specific contracts rather than transact on the market. In other words, even when the market can function it may be economical to ignore the market and enter into contracts instead.

In general, for certain types of activities within the firm, cost reduction is possible by supplanting the market and introducing the contractual mode of organization. It should be observed that given a demand curve for the product of the firm the management may be motivated to introduce the cost saving contracting process in its desire to maximize profits. Concurrently, the cost reductions so obtained have the effect of increasing consumer welfare. A mixed mode of organization, involving both markets and contracting, may be beneficial to the society.

There are some situations in which the market may not materialize at all. For instance, in the early stages of a product market there may be insufficient market for parts, spares and so on to the point where it is not economical to market them independently. Even in such cases contractual arrangements are necessary to economize on costs.

In the context of modern manufacturing technologies and large organizations it is likely that specific skills required by the firm can be best acquired within the firm and by the process of learning by doing. A manager confronted with a situation of this nature may almost always find that obtaining the requisite personnel on an internal contracting process is superior to recruitment on the market.

In view of such considerations Williamson (1979) noted that contracts will become necessary if

(a) markets cannot function either because the market demand is low or because there are bilateral monopoly bargaining stalemates created by asset specificity,

(b) market can function but is inefficient due to transaction costs or uncertain market demand,

(c) there is a critical input the market for it may develop monopoly power and exploit the producers of final output by claiming an asymmetrically large share of the profit or surplus that can be generated by the output producer,

(d) asymmetric information with agents in the exchange process may lead to exploitation in market exchange and some members may demand a contract, and

(e) the enforceable legal provisions of the contract can deter market exploitation and uncertainties.

1.4. INTERNAL ORGANIZATION

It has already been noted that the neoclassical theory of the firm assumes that all parties in the exchange have full and faultless information. It is also generally assumed that it is available to all the contracting parties at no cost. Even the coordination of inputs in the production process is assumed to be costless. However, in the context of the operation of imperfect markets the amount of information needed, the search costs, as well as the coordination problems cannot be underestimated.

In general, both contractual processes as well as market operations involve transaction costs over and above the prices paid for the inputs. These costs are a result of the need, on the part of the firm, to

(a) acquire information,

(b) draw up contracts, and

(c) monitor the execution of the exchange operations.

The firm may consider becoming self-sufficient by producing the requisite inputs with its own plant and machinery so long as the transaction costs are sufficiently high. Market induced transaction costs can be one of the reasons for internalization of certain operations within the firm.

A second reason for internalization has been the technological externalities in the process of executing certain tasks. When the externalities are significant the firm may have to undertake these tasks simultaneously to reap the cost advantages. In other words, organizing production of each of these tasks in different firms, even when it is feasible, may be relatively more expensive. The cost advantages of this nature can be organizational as well. Intra-firm competition, when it replaces the market, can bring about a cost reduction due to several factors:

(a) internalization harmonizes interests and permits an adaptive sequential decision process to be utilized,

(b) specific assets, in the form of better skills and learning by doing accrue to the firm. These assets enable the firm to process information expeditiously and at a lower cost.

Hence, the cost advantages of such internalizing in firms consist of both technological economies as well as those accruing from organizational design.

Just as technological and/or organizational externalities arise in doing many tasks so they can when producing several types of output. The cost complementarity implied in this description may induce firms to integrate production of two or more outputs. Such an expansion to a multiproduct firm can also be looked upon as internalization.

Multiproduct activities within the firm may arise even if there are no cost complementarities. In the process of dynamic evolution of a firm it may develop specific assets such as new product designs, new marketing abilities, and new technologies. And yet the firm may not be able to market these without jeopardising the profit generating opportunities of the existing product lines. The only alternative for the firm may be to integrate their production internally.

In imperfect markets expansion of the firm to multiproduct operations can also be induced by a very different set of conditions. It is well known that the market is limited relative to the technological economies of scale and that as a result excess capacity persists dynamically. In order to utilize the excess capacity, in its attempts to generate a larger profit, the firm expands into new lines of production. The difference between this case and the previous one is that the present situation arises even if cost complementarity does not exist. In other words, the internalization process may result in creating new demands for the firm's products as well.

1.5. ORGANIZATIONAL DESIGN

In the early stages of the firm there is no necessity for a formal organizational structure. The entrepreneur often carries out most of the business functions by himself. This is no longer possible and/or efficient as the firm grows. For, there is a necessity to link various related activities and exploit the principles of division of labor. In particular, in most of the modern manufacturing processes the number of operations involved as well as their complexity has increased. Under such conditions it was felt that breaking the production process into distinct modules and assembling them to obtain the final product is more efficient in the sense that greater output can be obtained from a given machine set up over a predefined interval of time.

In general, appropriate organizational structuring and design have been necessitated by various factors. In addition to the technological aspect alluded to here, there are other prominent factors; chief among them are

(a) the market transaction costs,

(b) limits on managerial abilities to process information, and

(c) the need to reduce opportunistic behavior of individuals within the firm.

The coordination of the various factor inputs and the identification of market opportunities from the sale of the output are important functions of any organization. This is the role of the management. Traditionally, however, economic theory attached too much importance to the notion that the economic performance and competitive conduct of the firm is the product of its position in, and the competitive structure of, external markets, and not enough to the possibility that internal organization may have a bearing upon these matters. A similar myopic attitude has resulted in many economists treating the development of the firm as being independent of internal structure whereas it is at least in part dependent upon internal structure.

So long as the firm confines itself to its original business areas, an U-form organizational structure will suffice. In particular, the firm will be divided up into functional departments dealing with buying, production, marketing, personnel, finance and the like. Coordination of the different departments is achieved through a board of directors which normally consists of the heads of the functional units.

It is by now evident that there is considerable scope for varying the extent to which different activities are brought within the control of a single organization (vertical integration), rather than bought in from separate suppliers as and when required. The functional organization begins to show serious signs of weakness once the firm reaches that stage of corporate development where it begins to grow by diversifying into new business areas. For, single functional departments within the firm, such as sales and finance departments, find themselves having to deal with several distinct businesses. This increases work load, results in a loss of information, and make coordination of individual business activities across departments difficult. The organizational response to these problems has generally been to replace the original functional structure and reassemble the firm into a new decentralized firm based upon product divisions (M-form). Each product division deals with a conceptually different business and is basically self-contained with its own functional hierarchies.

Such an integrative process is at work in the emergence of complex organizations. Concurrently, there have been practical compulsions to decentralize and divisionalize jobs.

(a) dividing the organization into natural decision making units (minimizing the between unit interaction) has been found to be attractive in practice whenever the overall tasks are large and complex. Chandler (1962, 1977) noted that a divisional or M-form structure based on product lines was more important in the development of certain organizations. In some cases, where the level of technology is high, functional specialization based on specific tasks (U-form structure) has been considered essential. A detailed discussion is availabe in Burton and Obel (1984, Ch. 4). In general, the specialized firm has a functional structure and the diversified company has a divisional structure.

(b) when the organization grows in size the decision making process becomes complex. The information, which is necessary for making effective decisions, will not be available to any one person. At the same time, an all channel network of communications (between each of the individuals in the organization and all the others) would be inefficient and counter productive. Consequently, specialization and division of labor takes the form of market related or functional areas of specialization.

(c) individuals, even when they recognize the necessity for cooperation, will be fundamentally oriented toward private gains. Thus, when individual performance in a group cannot be measured and/or monitored adequately, they will tend to shirk work and act as free-riders on the group to which they belong. Similarly, individuals would find that not reporting (to the group) all the information they have, either regarding production or markets, can be advantageous to themselves. Even this moral hazard problem can be reduced only by divisionalization and forming groups of like minded people.

These difficulties indicate that divisionalization of the activities of the organization arises as a practical necessity while integrating the common interests of a larger group. Planned coordination of collective activities of individuals, functioning on a relatively continuous basis through division of labor and hierarchy of authority, is an imperative for the attainment of organizational goals.

Roughly speaking, as Radner (1986) puts it, the subunits of the firm are to two types:

(a) cost centers, and

(b) profit centers.

As the terms suggest, a profit center has some profit imputed to it in each accounting period. The cost centers have the responsibility of organizing the acquisition and utilization of resources to produce a planned level of output. Generally, a budget will be allocated to a cost center and its manager has to deliver the expected outputs within this budget.

Three aspects of such organizations make the problem of allocating resources and coordinating activities within a firm difficult.

(a) There are no market prices to direct activities within a firm. The requisite activities will have to be performed and coordinated by the visible hand of management at various levels.

(b) Managers and workers at different levels in the hierarchy will have specialized information or expertise concerning particular spheres of activity. Usually this information is not available to other individuals within the firm including top management.

(c) Individuals with private information also have interests which may diverge from those of the firm and may find it disadvantageous to reveal their privileged private information to the management. The differences in the objectives and the general nature of the moral hazard was initially identified in the financial context by Berle and Means (1968) and was emphasized in the literature on the principal-agent problem which was systematically formulated by Jensen and Meckling (1976).

In essence, as Hariss et al. (1982) emphasized, both

(a) the asymmetry of information at various levels of management, and

(b) the differences in the motiviations and objectives of workers at different levels of hierarchy, will have to be accepted as a reality in the decision making process.

From a practical viewpoint what the management can do is to choose an allocation of resources, which is optimal from their vantage-point, keeping in perspective the information they have about the lower levels of heirarchy. However, such an allocation may not be optimal in the presence of asymmetric information since it fails to exploit the more complete information available at the lower levels of hierarchy. It may not be consistent with the expectations of the lower levels either. The alternative available to them is to delegate decision making with respect to production organization and certain other details to the lower levels of heirarchy. The lower levels may, in turn, utilize favorable information advantages to exploit the higher level of management. But they experience an information asymmetry with respect to markets and the profit position. This can result in inefficient decisions. Hence, in either case, the concept of an efficient resource allocation as well as the process through which it can be achieved are in doubt.

It is therefore essential to define the organizational structure, the information and monitoring systems, the incentive mechanisms and the decision rules (contractual processes) in order to ascertain the degree to which the divergent interests of the different groups in the organization can be satisfied. Stated somewhat differently, signalling by subunits, information flows across subunits, monitoring of activities, as well as the incentives offered to different subunits can be said to affect the economic behavior within organizations.

Thus, as Knight (1951, p. 22) remarked, organizations have a comparative advantage in situations where uncertainty is large and information difficulties exist. But the construction and operation of organizations is costly. In particular, the larger an organization grows, the greater in proportion is the amount of resources and effort that must be expended in merely holding it together.

1.6. NATURE OF THE STUDY

For a very long time there has been a feeling that the conventional theory of the firm does not portray the features encountered in real life sufficiently adequately to understand its behavior. Perhaps, to an extent, the preoccupation of economic theory of the firm with efficiency of market performance justified the emphasis on the structure of markets as a source of inefficient performance. Given the market conditions, the internal organization and management of the firm itself is expected to be always efficient. However, the large modern corporations are such that the owners (shareholders) do not really have an effective control on the management of the firm. Partly this is a result of the emerging financial structures and the resultant diffusion of ownership. It has also been recognized that the sheer size of the enterprise and the degree to which vertical integration reduces market transactions can place a limit on the efficient management of the firm. The relevant question is: what are the criteria and conditions to ensure efficient internal functioning of the firm? Stated differently, given an organizational structure, when can the internal decision process of the management be considered as efficient? The relative efficiency of different organizational forms themselves need careful analysis. In both these types of studies the market itself is assumed to be monopolistic competition so that the emphasis shifts from the efficiency of market organization to that of the efficiency of the internal decisions of a single firm within the market.

Once this change in emphasis and the necessity for it is recognized the problem can be structured along conventional lines. The important aspects are:

(a) what is the relevant list of variables which the firm can choose from?,

(b) what is the choice set availabe to the firm?, and

(c) what are the criteria on the basis of which choices are made and/or ought to be made?

The preoccupation of the economic theorist is always on the maximization of welfare of the community of which the firm is a part. Several attempts are being made to examine this micro level behavior of firms. This shift of emphasis in the theory of the firm has been as enduring as it has been arduous.

Strictly speaking the detail at which orgnaizational and institutional structures differ can be bewilderingly complex. Further, the differences among them would be such that discrete choice problems would be involved. Both the conceptual apparatus and the computational procedures tend to be difficult. When so many complex issues are involved it is natural to make an attempt to identify the most significant dimensions and the interactions among them before embarking on any analysis. In this process the well-known criticism that what is not included in the analysis may turn out to be far more important than what is can never fully be avoided. Even so the analysis has to proceed in steps albeit of increasing relevance and perforce of greater complexity.

In the initial stages of organizational economics attempts were made to examine the implications of the differences in the managerial motivations in the process of decision making and it appears to be clear that no generalization is ever possible. Detailed studies of the many likely patterns is still in progress.

At the second stage the design of organizations in terms of task specific and/or function specific allocation and management of workforce has been considered. An efficient design can be construed given a theory of behavior among organizations. Similarly, given the organizational design and the motivation of the individuals within it, a specific set of decision rules relating to expected or desirable behavior can be drawn up. Many of these variations are being considered elaborately but they have been so far confined to organizational aspects only.

The interaction of the organizational/institutional detail on the performance of the firm across markets is as yet not understood very well. Basically the organization theorist has not been interested in this dimension and the economist is as yet unable to redefine the conceptual apparatus necessary to move in this direction. Even so it is true that some attempts are being made especially in the context of information processing within a firm and market, product choice in monopolistic competition, and the ownership structures in the theory of finance.

There is a feeling that running through the entire gamut of these problems is a necessity to define efficient choices of some generic concepts of internal decisions of firms. Corresponding to each classification there will perhaps be a different set of efficiency rules. If this can be set up the analytical problems can perhaps be structured. The concepts of X-efficiency appeared to promise a movement in this direction. But the micro-micro level emphasis of Leibenstein (1980, 1987) was too ambitious and the resulting efficiency notions are at best ambiguous. In a way therefore the initial attempts at such a quantum jump in the theory of the firm were abortive.

A somewhat restricted, albeit concrete and empirically deterministic, progress can be made if the set of internal decisions is confined to well defined entities which usually appear in a balance sheet and profit and loss account of the firm. After all the theories of industrial economics and industrial organization which had this type of focus could yield concrete results. But this level of generalization has not been attempted in the context of organizational economics. A beginning will be made in this direction.

At a deeper level the compulsions for the design of efficient organizations and internal decisions may themselves depend crucially on the nature of the markets. The converse is perhaps true as well. For, the efficiency with which an organization can deal with internal decisions may place a limit on the size of the firm and consequently determine the number of firms in a market. It would be the essence of organizational economics to capture these interactions.

One of the expected tangible gains would be in the proper identification of even the allocative efficiency concepts associated with different market forms in the theory of the firm. For, it is by now evident that organizational structures do have a bearing on the determinants of the cost functions and their properties. Stated differently, the allocative efficiency in a given market depends both on the organization and the internal environment of the firm as well as on the structure of markets. Disentangling these two dimensions may contribute significantly to a study of the economics of organizational design.

In the final analysis one should not expect to find a unique optimal solution to organizational design, structure of internal decisions, and consequently conduct and performance on market structures which are themselves evolving endogenously. Instead there will be many undominated equilibria resembling the Pareto optimal market allocations and further value judgements will spring up. It is rather difficult to visualize the likely nature of these issues but progress in this direction appears to be warranted. The dynamic disequilibria and the transitions to preferred states are easily the essence of any practical and usuable approach to organizational economics. The ultimate efficient equilibria, even if they can be defined, have limited value in comparison to the analysis of transitional dynamics.

CHAPTER 2

WELFARE AND INEFFICIENCY

2.1. THE MANAGERIAL MILIEU AND WELFARE

In neoclassical economic theory the firm has three distinct features:

(a) it is a one person organization,

(b) the manager is also the owner of all the physical and financial assets of the firm and property rights enable him to be a claimant of all the residual profits in its operation, and

(c) all the input and output transactions are conducted through the market mechanism. In the case of certain lines of production the economical size of the firm is large and the organization becomes increasingly complex. Even in such a context neoclassical theory assumes that the organizational structure and the incentive mechanisms, provided to the workers at different levels of heirarchy, will be designed in such a way that the firm can be managed as if it is a one person affair.

Within the framework of such a theory of the firm it is generally postulated that consumer soverignity, as reflected in the demand curves which they exhibit[1], will have to be satisfied while organizing production. In particular, social welfare is defined as the utility generated, by the volume of output produced and exchanged on the market, net of social costs. It is also assumed that the society would seek to maximize net social welfare. Such a behavior is expected to be independent of the nature of the markets for inputs and outputs. Though this definition of economic

---

[1] Dobb (1969, pp. 5ff) presented an excellent analysis on this aspect of the specification of social welfare.

welfare is not universally accepted it remains at the apex of almost the entire analytical work in the thoery of the firm.

In such a context the important analytical question relates to the extent to which self-seeking agents in market exchange enable the system to attain maximum social welfare. Since the consumer preferences are assumed to be given exogenously the result would depend upon the decision making process of the owner manager. In the context of market exchange the owner manager, who has the property rights, can be expected to organize production so as to maximize the profits which will accrue to him as payment for the specific assets which he owns. Even in the case of large firms with complex organizational structures the assumption of profit maximization is retained and their performance is expected to be similar to the one person owner manager enterprise within a given market environment. Based on such a generalization, attempts have been made to show that both the consumers and the firms, acting independently and in their own interest and exchanging goods and services on the market, contribute to social welfare as well.

However, Hicks (1935) pointed out that even in the context of one person organizations the owner manager may value effort along with profits and deviate from profit maximization in the decision making process. The difference in the ownership and management in large organizations, emphasized by Berle and Means (1968), reinforced this viewpoint. In particular, diffused ownership would mean that the manager does not necessarily receive even a share of the profit which he evaluates as being commensurate with his efforts. Consequently, the manager may not be motivated to maximize profits. Instead, they may develop policies in such a way as to shelter themselves from takeover threats by generating adequate profits and pursue their own preferences. Similarly, it was recognized by Penrose (1959), Teece (1982) and others that some workers within the organization may develop specific skills which become fixed assets of the firm over time. One of the consequences of the phenomenon, as Scherer (1980) pointed out, is that they may develop bilateral monopoly powers vis a vis the owner manager. As a result, these specific assets would begin to claim a part of the residual. The motivation, of the owner manager, to maximize profits tends to be weaker. The behavioral theories of the firm sought to model different types of managerial preferences that are likely to emerge and their consequences for the performance of the firms.

One further aspect of the structure and conduct of large firms was also emphasized. As the organization becomes complex and the number of heirarchical levels increases there is a possibility of the owner manager losing control due to what Williamson (1971) described as information impactedness[2]. The motivational patterns of owners and managers at different levels of heirarchy may then add up to certain observed behavior. It was claimed by Leibenstein (1980), among others, that the detailed motivational patterns should be examined to appropriately design and appraise performance of complex organizations. Hoenack (1983) made an attempt to develop an economic theory of behavior within organizations. Extensive analytical work on various alternatives to market organization is in progress.

It was also quite clear, starting with the work of Chamberlin (1962), that when confronted with the problems of survival the management may be motivated to adopt nonprice strategies to insulate itself against competition. Such strategies can have wide ranging effects on the performance of the firm and social welfare. The effects of advertising on welfare alone

---

[2] Primarily, information impactedness represents the lack of adequate information to monitor production efficiently.

have been systematically examined so far.

In general, welfare economics tends to dichotomize the sources of inefficiency into

(a) market related or allocative, and

(b) those induced by managerial motivations.

Market related inefficiencies are generally attributed to the changes in the elasticity of the demand curve for the products of any one firm resulting from the small number of firms in the market. Similarly, from an analytical viewpoint it may be quite simple to conjecture that managerial motivations have a fundamental bearing on the cost structure of the firm and consequently on economic welfare. Liebenstein (1966) emphasized this viewpoint. However, it is not always clear that managerial inefficiency develops only as a result of certain preferences they exhibit. It is also not conclusively established that managerial motivations do alter the costs of production[3]. Further, even when managerial preferences alter the costs of production, the welfare effects induced by alternative forms of managerial preferences as well as the channels through which such choices result in welfare loss remained elusive.

The primary purpose of this chapter is to set out the issues involved in their essential detail and place emerging concepts in perspective. It appears that most of these analytical details carry over, albeit with suitable changes, in the context of welfare economics of nonprice strategies, design

---

[3] The necessity to minimize social costs, in attempts to maximize social welfare, has been explicitly stated in much of the literature. See, for instance, Dobb (1969, pp. 54ff). The necessity for such a requirement can be appreciated by recalling that in the presence of external diseconomies in production the social cost exceeds the private cost. However, the owner manager of the firm, who is inclined to take only the private costs into account in his decision making process, may generate a higher level of output in comparison to the social optimum. Coase (1960) brought the distinction between private and social costs into prominence in such an analysis. A useful analysis concerning the losses in social welfare inflicted by such external diseconomies can be found in the recent work of Shilony (1983). This aspect of the problem should be emphasized even in the organizational context.

of incentive mechanisms, as well as other internal decisions of complex organizations. It would be helpful to delimit these notions clearly in a simple framework before proceeding with the greater complexity inherent in the analysis of the functioning of complex organizations. Inevitably the exercise envisaged here results in raising certain conceptual issues which should receive greater attention.

2.2. THE NEOCLASSICAL PARADIGM

The concept of social welfare is generally built up by considering the net gains to the consumers and the producers in the process of production and exchange. The essential underpinnings can be exhibited by considering these net gains sequentially.

The notion of the net gain to the consumer is ususaly developed through the idea of consumer surplus. It is generally argued that the consumer chooses the quantities of different commodities he purchases in such a way as to make the marginal utility from an additional unit of the commodity proportional to the price paid for it. The factor of proportionality is the marginal utility of income and, if units of measurement of the quantities of the commodities purchased are properly chosen, the area under the demand curve can represent the total utility to the consumer[4]. Hence, the total utility less the cost of purchasing the desired units of output can be used as a measure of the consumer surplus. In Fig.2.1 the area $p_1 AB$ represents the consumer surplus for the output level Y_1.

---

[4] One of the basic postulates of this theory is that the demand curve revealed by the consumer in market exchange is socially desirable. This is usually the implication of consumer sovereignity. Occasionally, questions have been raised about the social desirability of certain types of consumption even if the consumers are willing to pay for them. This aspect does not however receive any prominence in much of the literature.

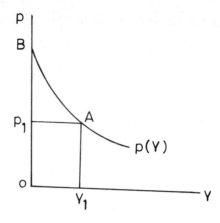

Figure 2.1. Consumer Surplus

In the context of a one person owner manager organization it would appear reasonable to argue that the revenue generated in the market exchange of a given level of output net costs is the measure of net gains to the producer. Referring to Fig.2.2 observe that for the level of output

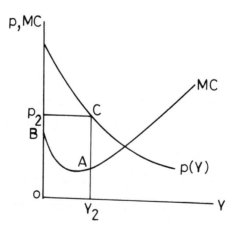

Figure 2.2. Neoclassical Welfare

Y_2 the firm obtains a revenue equal to the area OY_2Cp_2 whereas the cost of production is represented by the areaOY_2AB under the marginal cost curve. The difference, area $BACp_2$, is the producer surplus. Further, given the property rights, the producer surplus accrues to the owner manager of specific assets and/or the fixed factor as rents[5].

The concept of social welfare must be appropriately specified even after the net gains of the two parties in the exchange process have been identified seperately. The sum total of the consumer and producer surplus is generally considered as an adequate measure of social welfare if such an aggregate index is necessary. For, referring to Fig.2.2, the level of output Y_2 is such that the additional utility Y_2C is generated at a managerial cost Y_2 resulting in an increase in social welfare given by AC. This value judgement is often imposed in concretizing the analysis[6]. Since

$$W(Y) = \text{total surplus or aggregate welfare}$$
$$= \int_0^Y p(y)dy - C(Y)$$

it follows that the welfare maximizing level of output, Y_w, satisfies the equation

$$p(Y_w) = MC(Y_w)$$

---

[5] A lucid exposition of these concepts and the difficulties associated with them can be found in Currie et al. (1971) and Mishan (1981, Ch. 5).

[6] Two considerations are generally taken into account in arriving at this conceptualization.

  (a) Social welfare increases so long as one of the parties in the exchange can gain without the other party losing.

  (b) If there is an overall gain, even with one of the parties experiencing a reduction in net surplus, it may be possible to set up compensation mechanisms to enhance social welfare. These ideas have been succintly stated in Dobb (1969, pp. 11ff, pp. 47ff).

where MC is the marginal cost of production. This is represented in Fig.2.3[7].

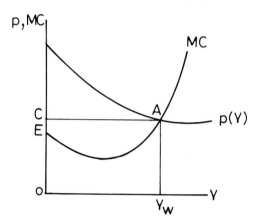

Figure 2.3. Welfare Maximum

Notice that the specification of Y_w does not depend on the nature of the product market. Further, the allocation of gains between the consumers and the producers is left implicit[8]. Another important aspect of the specification remained implicit in the above description. Conceptually, the net addition to the welfare of the society from the production of a unit of output is the highest if the factors of production are chosen, for given input prices, so as to minimize the social cost of production. In general, this is one of the first requirements of welfare maximization.

---

[7]It should be noted that Y_w does not maximize producer surplus when the product market is not competitive. The owner manager is only a residual claimant in the operation of the market mechanism.

[8]In much of the neoclassical theory the distribution of gains is assumed to be determined by the market mechanism. Such a distribution is Pareto optimal in the usual sense though it is not unique. Very few attempts have been made to redefine Y_w based on explicit compensation criteria. Distributional or equity considerations are generally implicit in neoclassical formulations.

Consider the actual choices of the firm in the operation of a specific market. It would be necessary to examine

(a) the input choices for a given level of output, as well as

(b) the choice of the level of output. With respect to the first, it can be readily verified that so long as the management maximizes profit the minimum cost choices of inputs will prevail[9].

For, given a level of output Y,

$$\pi(Y) = \text{ profit of the firm}$$
$$= Yp(Y) - C(Y)$$

and, in its endeavor to maximize π, the only choice available to the management is to organize the production of Y in such a way as to minimize $C(Y)$ since $p(Y)$ is determined exogenously by the market. However, it is well known that the profit maximizing choice of output (Y_π) of a monopolistic firm does not maximize welfare. With a downward sloping demand curve and the usual cost curves the welfare and profit functions will have inverted U-shapes as shown in Fig.2.4. Further, at the welfare maximizing level of output (Y_w), marginal revenue is less than price which in turn is equal to the marginal cost. Consequently, the profit maximizing level of output Y_π is less than Y_w. The primary source of this inefficiency is the inelasticity of demand. For, as Spence (1977) noted,

$$Y_\pi p(Y_\pi) = \text{ revenue generated}$$
$$= [1 - (\frac{1}{\eta})] \int_0^{Y_\pi} p(y)dy$$

---

[9] It is being assumed, for the present, that there are no external economies or diseconomies in production.

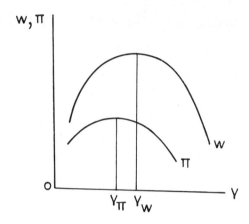

Figure 2.4. Welfare vs. Profit Maximum

where η is the elasticity of demand. From this it can be concluded that a lower elasticity will not enable the firm to convert consumer utility into profit. Competitive product markets alone would be such that welfare maximum can be attained. For, in that case, the W and π curves coincide.

It is essentially this observation which leads to the conclusion that the market structure itself, rather than the nature of managerial preferences, constitutes the source of inefficiency and welfare loss. Allocative inefficiency is a result of product market imperfection. It reduces the benefits to the consumers as well as the producers[10].

---

[10] Conceptually the social welfare loss and inefficiency is an abstract concept. It gets to be recognized and expressed in public forums only if one or both of the parties in exchange explicitly identifies it. In the present context, since there is a reduction in consumer as well as producer surplus it is relatively simple to argue that it will be recognized and explicitly expressed. The situations where only the consumers have a loss have generally been much more difficult to recognize. They do not receive a wider acceptance and the necessity for appropriate corrective action is under estimated. Pollution control and environmental decay have been outstanding examples in recent times. Even the concepts of consumerism belong to this category. The corporate economy tends to provide a much greater economic power to the management and consumer sovereignty is not easily attainable.

2.3. THE BAUMOL FIRM

Baumol (1959) noted that the only major requirement on managerial behavior, in the corporate environment characterized by the seper-
ation of ownership and control, is to ensure that a certain mimimum
profits is generated so that shareholders are content and takeover bids
are avoided. The actual level of profits which can be attained at Y_π in
Fig.2.4 will generally exceed the minimum requirement. The existence of
these excess or discretionary profits[11] gives rise to the possibility that the
managers would utilize discretionary profits to attain other objectives. In
the original Baumol framework the additional profits are traded off to
increase sales and create a more stable market for the firm. For, it was
argued that doing so would benefit the management by improving job
security and providing a greater scope for exercising their powers.

Somewhat more generally, the behavioral theories of the firm acknowledged the possibility that the management of the firm may value
size per se and maximize a utility function of the form $U(\pi, Y)$; $U_1 >
0$, $U_2 > 0$. The consequences of such managerial preferences for social
welfare can be identified. Note that, as in the previous section, U can be
increased, for a given Y, only through π and the cost function in turn.
Since $U_1 > 0$ it can once again be expected that the firm would choose
inputs in such a way as to minimize costs of production. However, it
is evident from Fig.2.5 that inefficiency may persist due to the output
choice. Two distinct points should be noted:

(a) $Y_\pi < Y_u < Y_w$ even if in efficiency persists. Further, $Y_u > Y_w$ need
not be ruled out. Even this can be viewed as a manifestation of an
inefficient choice of the level of production.

---

[11] This expression is due to Williamson (1964). However, as Odagiri (1981) remarked,
it is generally assumed that the minimum required profit is given to the management
exogenously.

(b) In the present context the difference between W_m and W_π is economic inefficiency created by the product market whereas there is a gain in efficiency from W_π to W_m due to managerial preferences. Similarly observe that even in competitive markets, where W and π coincide, the existence of a utility function of the form $U(\pi, Y)$ results in $Y_u > Y_w$ and consequently some reduction in social welfare. Managerial preferences, rather than the nature of the product markets, are the source of welfare loss represented by $W_m W_u$.

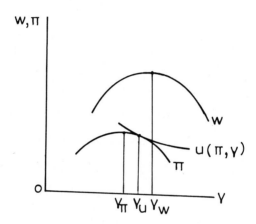

Figure 2.5. The Baumol Firm

An alternative theory considers the possibility that, within the bounds of survival, the managers will regard the expansion of the firm as creating a personal cost. For example, the disutility of effort involved in expansion may be considered as disproportionate to the expected share of profits. In such a case the managers may trade off certain profits in order to reduce the disutility of managerial effort. U_2 will then be negative. However, the input choices of the firm would still be such as to minimize the cost for a given Y. The only difference is the choice of the level of output. As depicted in Fig.2.6, Y_u will now be lower than Y_π. The welfare loss from

W_π to W_u cannot be considered as a welfare loss. This can be examined most clearly in a situation in which the product market is competitive but the managerial preference function is of the form $U(\pi, Y)$. For, in competitive markets, output level Y_w would be such that

$$U_1[p(Y) - MC(Y)] + U_2 = 0, \quad \text{or}$$
$$MC(Y) = p(Y) + (U_2/U_1).$$

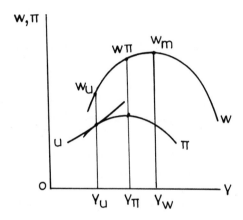

Figure 2.6. Managerial Behavior and Welfare

In such a case, referring to Fig.2.7, it can be claimed that the reduction in output from Y_w to Y_u is entirely due to the managerial preferences. However, the producers, given their utility function, may feel that they have received a more than adequate compensation for the loss in producer surplus. But they have inflicted a loss in welfare to the consumers equivalent to the area $ABED$ which is the reduction in the consumer surplus for the observed reduction in output. The area $ABED$ is managerial inefficiency. This is the only meaningful interpretation within the neoclassical scheme because the producers can only be residual claimants and not have first

34

priority on the share of welfare accruing to them[12].

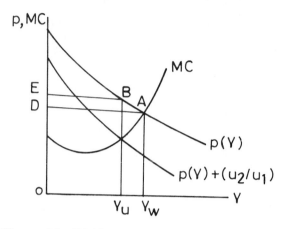

Figure 2.7. Welfare Loss Due to Managerial Choice

The case of imperfect product markets is analogous. Consider Fig.2.8. A reduction of Y from Y_π to Y_u entails a loss in welfare equal to the area $ABJK$. A portion of this, namely the area $EBAD$ represents the loss in consumer surplus while $EBHD - HAKJ$ represents the change in producer surplus. However, since the management is willing to trade off producer surplus and profit for the reduction in the disutility derived from a smaller Y, the only loss is to the consumer. Hence, whereas the consumer would like to see at least Y_π maintained he is unable to enforce it given the managerial preferences. That is, even if it is acknowledged that Y_u is a disequilibrium configuration, the consumer is entitled to complain that there is a loss in welfare equivalent to the area $EBAD$. This is a

---

[12]It can perhaps be argued that in the present disequilibrium situation the producers will bargain with the consumers, compensate them for the loss, and preserve the maximum net social welfare. However, as has been pointed out earlier, the management would not acknowledge the existence of inefficiency and the welfare loss since it is not in their interest to do so. Even in cases where such an acknowledgement is forthcoming and compensation is contemplated, there are practical difficulties in arriving at appropriate compensation rules. These have been recently highlighted by Knetch and Sinden (1984) and Marshall (1986).

measure of managerial inefficiency.

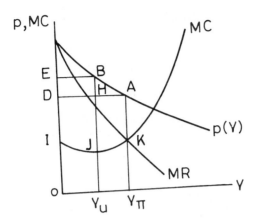

Figure 2.8. Imperfect Markets and Welfare Loss

However, it is possible to argue that the neoclassical aggregate welfare measure does not explicitly recognize the distribution of welfare between the producers and the consumers. If so, the loss in consumer surplus alluded to above will have to be weighed against the utility gains to the producer. If there is a net reduction in the overall utility level as output is reduced from Y_π to Y_u then, and only then, can any notion of managerial inefficiency be sustained. This approach to the problem depends on the interpretation that the neoclassical welfare procedures assign equal weights to the producer and consumer utilities in arriving at the aggregate measure of social welfare.

Gravelle (1982), for instance, proposed the alternative of weighting the consumer surplus appropriately and adding it to the managerial preference function to obtain the measure of aggregate welfare. This approach can be shown to alter the inferences regarding the notions of managerial inefficiency and its occurence in the operation of monopolistic product markets.

Let the welfare of the society be defined by

$$W(Y) = \lambda[\int_0^Y p(y)dy - Yp(Y)] + U(\pi, Y)$$

where λ can be interpreted as the marginal utility of a unit of income to the consumers. For expository convenience it will be assumed to be a constant independent of the level of income. The welfare maximizing level of output Y_w satisfies the equation

$$MC(Y_w)[1 - (\frac{1}{\eta}) + (\frac{\lambda}{U_1})] + (\frac{U_2}{U_1}) = p^*(Y_w)$$

where $U_1 = \partial U/\partial \pi$, and $U_2 = \partial U/\partial Y$. Consider the case where $U_2 < 0$ in order to appreciate the deviation of the management decisions regarding Y from the efficient level. Assume further that $p^*(Y) < p(Y)$. Then, it can be verified from Fig.2.9(a) that $Y_w^* < Y_w$. Similarly, the choice of the management would be such that $Y_u < Y_w^*$. This can be readily inferred from Fig.2.9(b).

As before, this result can be contrasted with that which obtains under the assumption of competitive product markets. Note that in this case

$$W(Y) = U(\pi, Y).$$

Consequently, $Y_w = Y_w^*$ is restored. In other words, the observed deviation between Y_u and Y_w^*, represented in Fig.2.9, is entirely due to the market imperfection. The concept of managerial inefficiency is no longer tenable since Y_w and Y_π are not relevent for analysis under the revised definition. Alessi (1983), in particular, argued that the concept of managerial inefficiency cannot be sustained if the managers, as decision makers, are free to pursue their objectives. This is the other extreme position in the

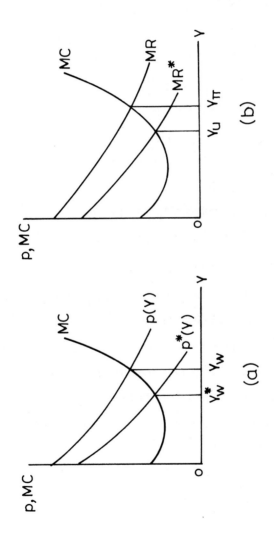

Figure 2.9. Alternative Welfare Assessment

literature. It would reflect producer sovereignty rather than what is usually claimed in neoclassical welfare economics about consumer sovereignty being at the center of analysis.

It is often made clear in the literature that the total social welfare is defined without any apriori considerations of the sharing between consumers and the producers. The only essential assumption is that the demand curves are exogenously given. The assumption that both the parties in exchange are free to pursue their preferences expressed in some other form is not essential to the definition of social welfare itself. Hence, this analytical construct is not in consonance with the notions of neoclassical welfare economics.

In the rest of the analysis it will be maintained that

(a) there is a welfare loss, to be designated as allocative inefficiency, due to the imperfection of the product market, and

(b) there is a welfare loss, equivalent to the reduction in consumer surplus, resulting from the managerial preferences.

The latter component corresponds to managerial inefficiency. Such an interpretation would be consistent with the traditions of neoclassical welfare economics. It is perhaps essential to emphasize the latter so that there is an explicit recognition for the necessity of conflict resolution mechanisms and compensatory principles. The consumer sovereignty arguments should again be at the apex of the development of such complementary instruments to market price.

2.4. EXTERNAL CONSTRAINTS AND FIXED COSTS

Williamson (1964) was the first to note that the management may distribute discretionary profits between staff expenditures, managerial perquisites and so on. That is, unlike the Baumol firm, which expands only along the output dimension, the behavioral theories postulate that even discretionary payments to factors of production and input choices may get to be valued by the management[13]. When managers exhibit such preferences there may be a shift in the cost curves as well as a change in the level of output chosen by the firm. Both these aspects of behavior have implications for welfare economics. Hence, an attempt must be made to identify the basic conceptual problems which necessitate analytical attention.

However, before proceeding with such an analysis it is essential to note that all cost changes reflected in the decisions of the management of the firm are not due to their volition alone. Instead, it is possible to show that certain cost changes are imposed on the management by the external environment and as such inefficiencies, if any, are still allocative and induced by factors other than managerial preferences. Situations are also conceivable wherein some cost changes, induced by discretionary managerial behavior, cannot have any impact on economic welfare. It will be useful to record these arguments before attempting any generalization.

Consider a situation in which the market for one or more of the factors of production is monopolistic. Under these conditions the firm experiences an increasing supply price and even the minimum attainable costs will be higher than those that would be necessary in the absence of such imperfection. To illustrate the argument, let x_2 be the variable factor in the production process and assume that the market for x_2 is

---

[13] There is an extensive literature on this aspect of the theory of the firm. Fairly comprehensive surveys can be found in Cyert and March (1965), Williamson (1964, 1967), Marris and Wood (1971), Hay and Morris (1979), and Gravelle and Rees (1981, Ch. 13).

such that

$$p(x_2) = \text{price per unit of } x_2$$

$$= p_2 x_2^{\alpha}; \quad \alpha > 0.$$

Let the production function of the firm be

$$Y = (x_1 x_2)^{1/2}$$

where x_1 is the fixed factor of production. Then, the short run cost of producing a given Y becomes

$$C^* = p_1 x_1 + p_2(Y^2/x_1)^{(1+\alpha)}$$

whereas the minimum cost would have been

$$C = p_1 x_1 + p_2(Y^2/x_1)$$

if the factor markets are competitive. Evidently, $C^* > C$ for all $\alpha > 0$. However, the firm could not have reduced costs below C^* given the external market environment.

It is possible to argue that the increase in marginal cost, induced by the imperfection of the factor markets, reduced output of even those firms which operate in a competitive market. As a result there is a reduction in output and a loss in total social welfare represented by the area $ABED$ in Fig.2.10. This will also be an aspect of allocative inefficiency analogous to the concepts developed earlier[14].

---

[14] Observe that the analysis of the welfare loss due to external diseconomies would be similar. However, in such a context it can be argued, as in the previous section, that the producers are willing to accept the loss in producer surplus since there is no way of capturing it in free market operations. Hence, only the amount $ALMB$, which represents the loss in consumer surplus, can be considered as the loss in social welfare.

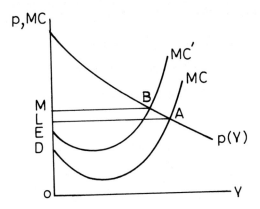

Figure 2.10. Cost Increase and Welfare

An alternative scenario was described by Cyert and March (1965). They contend that the members of the production team, who have the most accurate information regarding the excess profits earned by the firm in imperfect markets, may try to extract these gains and the owner and/or manager will have to accept organizational slack in their efforts to keep the firm stable. In terms of the foregoing example, the variable factor may extract a bonus such that

$$p_2(x_2) = (1 + \alpha)p_2; \quad \alpha > 0$$

so that the minimum cost of production becomes

$$C^* = p_1 x_1 + (1 + \alpha)p_2(Y^2/x_1).$$

It can be readily verified that $C^* > C$ for every level of output Y. Even in this case, the reduction in social welfare can be described only in terms of allocative inefficiency.

In most of the versions of the behavioral theories of the firm it is argued that the firm generates maximum profits but the organization apportions discretionary profits according to certain managerial preferences. Williamson's (1964, 1967) expense preference theory describes several such motivations. Some of these redistributions do not however affect social welfare in any fundamental way. To illustrate this argument assume that the perquisites or discretionary payments share of the profits is in the form of rent paid to fixed and/or specific assets of the firm. That is, there is merely a redistribution in the payments for the different fixed factors of the firm and no fundamental change in the determination of the variable costs. Expressed in terms of the above algebraic formalism

$$C^* = (p_1 x_1 + \beta \pi) + p_2(Y^2/x_1)$$

where $\beta \pi$ is the share of profits allocated to specific assets. So long as β is independent of x_1, that is profit allocation to specific assets is not proportional to the volume of their use, the calculation of economic efficiency remains invariant. See Fig.2.11. Hence, it follows that redistribution of profits and rents among the fixed factors and specific assets do not necessitate any new concepts of managerial inefficiency. Traditional costing conventions indicate that the overall costs of the firm have gone up but this, in itself, would not alter its performance. Such an analysis was explicitly recorded in Wood (1971, p.65).

Leibenstein (1980), and elsewhere, argued that the workers have their own motivational factors and the effort they put in may not be commensurate with the expectations of the mangers. Under these conditions the actual costs of producing a given level of output can exceed

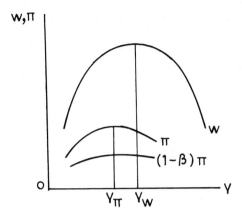

Figure 2.11. Discretionary Payments and Welfare

planned costs. Leibenstein considers this as a source of inefficiency generated by the operation of the firm rather than the market mechanism.
However, Williamson (1984) pointed out that idiosyncratic behavior of individuals cannot be considered as specific to any one organizational form
or managerial motivations. Instead, it is an external constraint in the
operation of the firm. In other words, cost increases of this nature, even
when they have been observed and acknowledged, cannot be designated
as managerial inefficiency. Instead, idiosyncratic behavior of this nature
is an intrinsic characteristic of the factors of production in the definition
of the social cost of providing goods and services on the market.

In general, the degree to which a manager can reduce the costs of
producing a given level of output through his choice of input combinations
ultimately depends upon the constraints that he faces. Some of these are
created by external market conditions, government control, and at any
point of time various external constraints placed on his abilities to obtain,
process, and utilize information generated by the given organizational

structure. Managerial inefficiency cannot arise so long as the managers are motivated to and actually develop decision rules to minimize costs and choose output levels to maximize social welfare within the overall limits set up by the external constraints. However, the question of which constraints are externally imposed on the management and which of them are due to their motivations and preferences cannot possibly be decided on any generalized objective criterion. This has been a source of some debate and misunderstandings in the literature.

2.5. DISCRETIONARY MANAGERIAL BEHAVIOR

It has been acknowledged earlier that the existence of excess profits may motivate the management to make discretionary payments to the factors of production. In the case of labor this may take the form of bonus, perquisites and so on. Basically such payments will result in an alteration of factor prices and changes in the cost of production even if cost minimization is followed thereafter. To illustrate this viewpoint, let the production function of the firm be

$$Y = (x_1 x_2)^{1/2}$$

p_1 price per unit of x_1,   and

$$p_2^* = p_2(1 + \alpha)$$

= market price plus discretionary payments per unit of x_2, where

αp_2 = bonus, prerequisites and so on per unit of x_2.

Cost minimizing input choices for a given Y result in the cost function

$$C^* = 2[p_1(1+\alpha)p_2]^{1/2}Y > C, \text{ since } \alpha > 0, \text{ where}$$

$$C = \text{ minimum cost in the absence of discretionary payments}$$

$$= 2(p_1 p_2)^{1/2}Y.$$

Hence, the movement from C to C^* represents an upward shift of the marginal cost curve. When the management confronts a strong labor union it may experience a disutility due to disruption of work, elaborate negotiations, the need to pay higher than market wages, and so on. Under these conditions the management may experience disutility of a larger workforce in addition to the cost implications. This can be represented by a managerial preference function of the form

$$U = C + \alpha x_2; \quad \alpha > 0$$

indicating a disutility for a higher C as well as x_2 choice. The management, which chooses x_1, x_2, for a given Y, so as to minimize U will utilize

$$x_1 = [p_1/(p_2+\alpha)]^{-1/2}Y, \quad x_2 = [p_1/(p_2+\alpha)]^{1/2}Y$$

and consequently the cost curve becomes

$$C^* = p_1^{1/2}Y[(p_2+\alpha)^{1/2}\{1 + p_2/(p_2+\alpha)\}]$$

which is greater than C for every value of Y since

$$(a-b)^2 > 0 \text{ where } a = (p_2+\alpha)^{1/2}, \text{ and } b = p_2^{1/2}.$$

Once again such managerial behavior invariably results in higher costs to the firm.

The disutility of a larger workforce can also be taken to manifest itself in the form of a preference for a greater degree of mechanization and larger capital stock. Suppose the management is postulated to maximize a preference function of the form

$$U = U(\pi, x_1); \quad U_1 > 0, \quad U_2 > 0.$$

Then, it is necessary to choose

(a) an appropriate x_1 for a given Y, and

(b) a value of Y which maximizes U.

Given the production function

$$Y = f(x_1, x_2),$$

and the choice of x_1 and the cost function can be developed in the following manner. From the production function there exists a choice of x_2 given by

$$x_2 = x_2(Y, x_1)$$

so that the cost function is

$$C = p_1 x_1 + p_2 x_2(Y, x_1).$$

Since the profit function is

$$\pi = Yp(Y) - p_1 x_1 - p_2 x_2(Y, x_1)$$

the utility maximizing choice of x_1 satisfies the equation

$$U_1[p_1 + P_2(\frac{\partial x_2}{\partial x_1})] = U_2.$$

From this the choice of x_1 can be implicitly written as

$$x_1 = x_1(Y, p_1, p_2).$$

Substituting this x_1 in C gives the cost function along which the firm operates. This will be denoted by $C^*(Y)$ and the corresponding marginal cost as $MC^*(Y)$. The increase in costs can be illustrated by utilizing the above example. Let

$$U = U(\pi, x_1) = \pi x_1.$$

Then, the choices of x_1 and x_2 will be

$$x_1 = pY/2p_1, \text{ and } x_2 = 2p_1Y/p, \text{ where}$$

$$p = \text{ price per unit of } Y.$$

Hence, the cost curve can be written as

$$C^* = (pY/2) + (2p_1p_2Y/p).$$

It can be readily verified that $C^* > C$ since $(p - 2a)^2 > 0$, where $a = (p_1p_2)^{1/2}$.

Leibenstein (1966) originally suggested this result. For, it was argued that in imperfect markets, where neoclassical motivations may not operate, there is a possibility that firms will be producing at a higher average cost. However, the implications of these cost changes for welfare analysis remained elusive.

Let the cost function along which the management operates be denoted by $C^*(Y)$. The management which maximizes $U(\pi, x_1)$ then chooses Y such that

$$MR(Y) = MC^*(Y) - (U_2/U_1)(\partial x_1/\partial Y).$$

Let Y_u be the level of output obtained by solving this equation. This is represented in Fig. 2.12. Even in the presence of product market

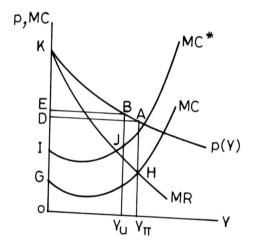

Figure 2.12. Cost Increase Due to Managerial Discretion

imperfection a profit maximizing management would have enabled society to derive a welfare level given by the area HGK. However, due to the discretionary managerial behavior being described here it is reduced to $BJIK$. The entire difference in the level of surplus was considered as a measure of managerial inefficiency in the original version of Leibenstein (1966) since managerial preferences are responsible for this welfare loss[15].

---

[15]In Leibenstein (1966, 1969, 1980) the marginal costs have been postulated to be constant for all values of Y. Hence, this interpretation takes on a connotation which will be closer to the argument which will be developed in the sequel. Leibenstein

However, it can be argued that the reduction in producer surplus, even if it occurs, is not a welfare loss since the management prefers it. A conflict arises only to the extent that the perceptions of the consumers are different from this. Notice that market imperfection alone would have reduced output to Y_π in Fig.2.12. However, the alternative managerial preferences result in its being reduced to Y_u. Thus, the area $ABED$ represents a loss in consumer welfare. The consumers can express it in market exchange or public policy forums even if they are not in a position to retrieve this welfare loss. It would therefore be legitimate to designate this as managerial inefficiency.

One alternative would be to argue that the total welfare be recomputed, after accounting for managerial preferences, and the welfare at Y_π compared to that at Y_u before drawing any inferences about managerial inefficiency.

The extreme arguement, as noted in Section 2.3, would be to suggest that the definition of social welfare needs reconstruction. Suppose it is defined as

$$W(Y) = \lambda[\int_0^Y p(y)dy - Yp(Y)] + U(\pi, x_1).$$

Then, the choices of x_1 generates the cost function $C^*(Y)$ and the welfare maximizing level of output Y_w^* satisfies the equation

$$MC^*(Y_w^*) = p^*(Y_w^*)$$

where $p^*(Y)$ was defined earlier in Section 2.3.

(1980), and elsewhere, shifted the emphasis of the analysis without coming to grips with these conceptual difficulties which are essentail to a basic understanding of the notions of managerial inefficiency.

For purposes of welfare analysis the basic modifications to Fig.2.9 are the replacement of MC by MC^* and the redefinition of Y_u. However, once again the concept of managerial inefficiency cannot be sustained. For, as before, $Y_u = Y_w^*$ will be restored if the product markets are competitive. The basic disagreement between the two approaches is in the acknowledgement of the reduction in Y and the consequent reduction in consumer surplus caused by the cost changes and the associated managerial preferences.

The analysis of this section can be summarized in the following manner. Once discretionary managerial behavior is acknowledged the costs of producton will exhibit changes whenever

(a) p_1, p_2 are altered, and/or

(b) there is an explicit preference for the use of either of the factors beyond that which is implied by their contribution to cost alone.

In the presence of such discretionary behavior, managerial inefficiency, in the form of a loss of consumer surplus, coexists along with the concept of allocative inefficiency. These notions will be consistent with, rather than being antagonistic to, the assumption that both the consumers and the managers of the firm are free to pursue their own objectives in the operation of market exchange.

2.6. MANAGERIAL INEFFICIENCY

It is by now clear that certain managerial preferences give rise to input choices which are not cost minimizing. This excessive cost implies a loss in consumer surplus which can logically be defined as managerial inefficiency. This arises over and above the allocative inefficiency implicit in the product market imperfection. Only those managerial preferences which do not alter the variable costs of production for a given level of output can be excluded from considerations of managerial inefficiency. These results have been developed under the assumption that all input output transactions are conducted through the market mechanism.

It was noted at the outset that both contractual arrangements as well as internal organization (such as the governance structure and incentive mechanisms) can be adopted in the design of complex organizations. Very often it is claimed that such coordination mechanisms are necessitated by the primary requirement of cost minimization and that functioning of the firms under the new dispensation cannot be inefficient relative to the market mode of operation. But, as Coase (1937) pointed out, the managerial responses to slack which is generated by cost reduction policies can be similar to those observed in the presence of discretionary profits. From the viewpoint of welfare economics it would therefore be realistic to argue that while the organizational innovations do contribute to increases in welfare relative to the market mode the maximum, corresponding to the alternative social cost, is not being attained. The concepts and sources of managerial inefficiency detailed above would carry over in this context as well.

Two basic questions emerge from this analysis.

(a) Would the neoclassical definition of social welfare remain adequate even in the context of the modern corporate economy? It cannot be claimed that managerial inefficiency does not exist until the issue of appropriate weighting of consumer and managerial preferences is settled. However, there is nothing inherent in the logic of the alternatives considered in the earlier sections to recommend one of them over the others.

(b) Whenever there is a conflict of interest between the two groups in market exchange and price changes alone cannot resolve the differences how can we examine the existence and efficiency of explicit organizational mechanisms so that social welfare can be redefined? This has rarely been attempted.

As a result, the neoclassical concepts of social welfare should remain the basic guideline for evaluating the performance of the markets as well as managerial preferences. The managerial inefficiency concepts would be necessary if and when the alternatives are clearly defined and implemented.

However, Williamson (1971,p.112) and Malmgren (1961) argued that defining the managerial efficiency concept in a very broad long run context and trying to enforce it at every point of time would be impractical. Instead, its use is only in disequilibrium configurations. This is at once the strength of the managerial inefficiency notions as well as its weakness.

CHAPTER 3

EFFICIENCY OF ORGANIZATIONAL DECISIONS

3.1. ORGANIZATION AND WELFARE

The theory of the firm acknowledges that as the firm grows in size there will be an emergence of

(a) diffused ownership and separation of ownership and control,

(b) nonprice competition dominating the operation of the market mechanisms and price strategies, and

(c) a complex internal organization supplementing the market mode as a management structure.

These aspects of the structure of the firms have important implications for their conduct and performance. One such issue relates to the economic efficiency of internal decisions of the firm as distinct from the efficiency in the operation of the market itself.

Neoclassical welfare economics requires that when the firm purchases all the inputs from the market the choice should be such as to minimize the cost of producing a given level of output. The minimum cost notions as well as their necessity in the context of welfare economics must be redefined when nonprice competition, contracting or internalization is taken into account. Similarly, it should be obvious that nonprice decisions affect the demand curves of the firm. Hence, it would also be necessary to define the nature of consumer preferences toward these organizational decisions and relate the changes in demand to the contribution to welfare. For, as Chamberlin (1962, p. 146) remarked, welfare maximum is attained only when the combined cost curve is the lowest and the demand curve is the greatest.

Welfare economics is also concerned with the conditions under which welfare maximum can be attained in the actual operation of firms. Neoclassical welfare economics established that the existence of property rights with the owner manager, which result in profit maximizing behavior, would be such as to minimize costs in the choice of inputs. The output levels chosen by the firm would be welfare maximizing only if the product markets are competitive. However, the operation of the imperfect markets do not invalidate cost minimization so long as the profit maximization postulate is maintained. The allocative inefficiency is only in the choice of the level of output[16].

There has been a tendency to approach welfare implications of organizational choice and nonprice competition from a similar perspective. For, upto this point in the literature it has been argued that features of the product market — such as the elasticity of demand, entry barriers, and the number of firms — will explain inefficiency in internal organization as well. It can, however, be shown that these aspects of the product market provide an insufficient explanation for the observed inefficiency. Instead, there is a possibility of behavior modification and change of motivations of the managers in complex organizations. Consequently, it appears that it will be necessary to examine features which are intrinsic to the internal organization of the firm so that the sources and deviations from efficient performance can be identified and measured.

Discretionary managerial behavior and its consequences for welfare in the choice of outputs in monopolistic competition has already been considered in Chapter 2. It appears that the concept is useful even in the context of defining the economic efficiency of nonprice decisions and

---

[16] For, as Spence (1977), and elsewhere, pointed out the firm cannot fully convert consumer surplus into profits if the market demand for the product is not perfectly elastic.

internal organizational choices. This will be systematized by developing the concept of internal pressure on the management. Consumer preference for nonprice decisions, to the extent they can express such preferences, may not be fully reflected in the market performance due to the differential reaction from the managements of different firms. A concept of external pressure can be developed to provide a generic specification of the welfare effects of shifts in demand originating from nonprice and organizational decisions.

3.2. INTERNAL PRESSURE AND COST

The tranquility of the neoclassical paradigm is disturbed if the implications of the emergence of mixed organizational modes are examined closely. Suppose the firm decides to produce one on the inputs, say I, internally. Then, the total cost curve can be written as $C(Y, I)$. Further, as Stigler (1976) pointed out, the neoclassical paradigm requires that the rest of the inputs be chosen to minimize the cost[17] of producing a given Y and I. However, note that this approach is not useful for welfare analysis. For, the above argument clearly indicates that even if the $C(Y, I)$ is the minimum cost for a given Y and I the consequences of internally producing I and the welfare maximizing choices of I are not defined as yet. Stigler brushed the problem aside due to a failure to recognize that the solution cannot be obtained by referring to the market valuation of I alone.

A simple analytical argument can be developed in the following manner. Referring to Fig.3.1, adapted from Coase (1937), let AC_m

---

[17]As Cheung (1983) and others noted, the consumer may not be in a position to express a preference for certain decisions of the firm. All such decisions will have to be brought into this format for welfare analysis.

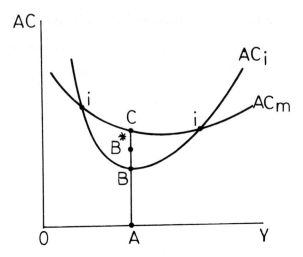

Figure 3.1. Costs of Internalization

represent the average cost of producing a given level of output Y when production is organized through the market and AC_i the average cost when I is produced within the firm[18]. Production of the input by the firm is then beneficial between the points marked as i. For, assume that A is the volume of output produced. AC is the average cost if the inputs are purchased on the market. AB is the minimum possible average cost if the production of I is internalized. The positive difference BC in the cost is primary motivation[19] for the internalization of the production of I. Hence, in general, the lowest point on the AC_i curve represents the welfare maximizing choice of I for a given Y.

Basic economic intuition therefore suggests that the logic of internal organization is quite distinct from that of the market. Consequently it

---

[18]It is as yet necessary to justify the U-shape of these curves. This will be examined presently.

[19]Other reasons for vertical integration and their implications for welfare will be examined in greater detail in Chapter 6.

appears that behavioral motivations which are intrinsic to the internal organization, are necessary to examine the efficient performance of the firm. The entire argument about the contribution to welfare of the internal decisions of the firm should be kept distinct from the choice of the output level itself. The analytical argument depends upon an appropriate specification of the costs in a specific organizational context.

The actual level of costs, which can be obtained for the given level of output A, will generally exceed the minimum AB possible. For, as in Chapter 2, it can be argued that the existence of the extra, or discretionary, profits in such an environment gives rise to the possibility that the management channels discretionary profits to attain other objectives.

This can be elucidated by referring to Fig.3.1. For, as Williamson (1964, p. 11) pointed out, when the difference BC is small and survival is narrowly bounded the management would approximate B. The organizational slack will then be low. If, however, BC is large, the managers may not be forced to initiate efficient action until the actual B^* obtained approaches C.

An attempt can now be made to show that the features related to the product market cannot be the explanation for such behavior in the functioning of these organizational forms. The inelasticity of demand in monopolistic markets, which is a result of the uniqueness of the product, is often considered as a source of monopoly power which reduces welfare. However, it is well known that in the long run group equilibrium, survival of the firm requires cost minimization for a given Y. Hence, the inelasticity of demand is inadequate to account for any reduction in welfare. Consider the possibility of defining the sources of inefficiency in terms of a reduction of the number of firms in the market. Such a reduction induces a shift in the demand curve to the right. But there is no reason for the profit maximizing firm to deviate from the minimum cost. Consequently, it cannot be claimed that there is no motivation to reduce costs of production. Hence, the reduction in the number of firms is also not a useful description as a cause of possible welfare loss. Thus, whatever may be the effect of the elasticity of demand and the number of firms on the market related inefficiency they cannot have any bearing on the efficiency of the internal organization of the firm. It is necessary to consider other features, intrinsic to the alternative organizational mode itself, to proceed with the analysis.

It is essential to recognize that the cost increases created by managerial choices and consequent welfare losses are at the apex of the analysis of the welfare changes brought about by nonprice competition and organizational decisions of the firm. This dimension adds to the neoclassical conceptualization of the inelasticity of demand in imperfect product markets as a source of allocative inefficiency.

The above description of the lack of internal pressure as one of the sources of welfare loss is subject to two qualifications. Firstly, the existence of managerial preferences of the form $U(\pi, I)$ do not necessarily eliminate the possibility of the welfare maximum of Y being attained even if it is by coincidence. Secondly, market imperfections, lack of property rights, or the absence of profit sharing incentive mechanisms do not automatically rule out the existence of internal pressure. It can only be claimed as a theoretical possibility. Its occurence in the actual operation of the firm remains an open question.

To sum up the analysis upto this point note that

(a) the choice of inputs to the production process and dimensions of nonprice competition may be the more fundamental changes brought about by the management,

(b) the existence of discretionary profits generated by the alternative organizational structure and separation of ownership from control are two major sources of behavior modification, and

(c) the effect of these choices on welfare is transmitted through the changes in the cost curves in addition to the output changes alluded to by Baumol (1959).

3.3 EXTERNAL PRESSURE AND EFFICIENCY

As noted earlier the major analytical problem in defining the economically efficient level of internal decisions is the lack of any explicit market valuation for them. In general, it is difficult to visualize the possibility of the consumer revealing preferences for all the decisions of the firm, even implicitly, to be reflected in the market price for the final output of the firm. Cheung (1983, pp. 8-9) puts it this way: when a consumer is buying a product there is an implicit payment for each component which goes into its production. But the consumers may not be able to place a valuation on each of these components for the simple reason that they may be interested only in the use of the commodity and they may not be aware of the role of each of the components in obtaining the service from the commodity.

In the context of a firm operating in a competitive market there is an unique price in the operation of such a market and the information is available to all the other firms as a free good. Further, there is sufficient pressure from the market to conform to the market price. On occasions, there can be imperfections in the product market. Constraints may also be imposed by government regulation. Under these conditions the market cannot exert sufficient pressure towards price equalization across firms. However, Leibenstein (1980, pp. 215-216) acknowledged that the management feels the market pressure so long as the price expected to rule for a given quantity of output is parametric whatever the market environment may be. This can be considered as the basic specification of external pressure.

Two factors must be considered explicitly to obtain an appropriate characterization of external pressure. Recall that every internal decision of the firm can leave an effect on the consumer choice and/or the reactions of the rival firms. External pressure can be said to exist if

(a) every one of the firms is fully informed about the choices of every other firm and they respond optimally, and

(b) the consumers have full information so that they precisely know the price they would pay for the product characteristics.

It is generally acknowledged that the firm may not consider competition along the price dimension to be the best alternative in its quest for obtaining maximum profits. Instead, nonprice competition may provide an effective shelter from competition. That is, the firm may be able to shift the demand curve to the right as a result of its decisions[20].

That is, as Leibenstein (1979, p. 18) pointed out, there is a possibility that a specific firm may enjoy a price differential in the market as a result of the "shelter the firm has created for itself." The strategies of product differentiation, advertising and so on belong to this category. Hence, the influence of the internal decision processes of the firm on its demand curve will have to be viewed as a fundamental specification of the lack of external pressure.

---

[20] From the consumer viewpoint
   (a) a fully vertically integrated firm may be a more reliable supplier of output when the markets for inputs are uncertain,
   (b) a firm which produces a range of complementary products may be more acceptable,
   (c) the products of a firm which advertises its goods may be deemed to be of better quality, and so on.

As with the definition of external pressure the lack of it may arise due to the inadequate reactions of the consumers and/or rival firms to specific nonprice decisions of a firm.

Consider a change in the quality of the product. The consumers will pay a price which is commensurate with their own valuation if they calibrate it through their own search process. However, the search process of the consumers cannot be costless. The firm may have a strategic advantage in such a milieu. For, even if they charge a price which is somewhat disproportionate to the improvement in quality, the consumers may pay for it if they feel that the search costs to evaluate the differences are higher. Thus increasing search costs, which the consumers confront, may be one of the reasons for the lack of external pressure from the consumers. Similarly, when the firm experiences increasing search costs in its efforts to delineate rival behavior, it may stop short of eliciting perfect information and may also react inadequately. Whenever this happens, each of the firms in the market may have an advantage over the rivals in their efforts to increase their own market demand. Such a situation signals lack of external pressure.

Assume, to begin with, that the firm experiences internal pressure and as a result maximizes profit. However, the lack of external pressure may be such that a choice of I which does not minimize the costs may yet result in a larger profit. That is, even when the firm is moving along the minimum cost curve for a given Y and I, the choice of I may be such that $C(Y, I)$ is not the lowest possible for a specific Y chosen by the firm. This has the effect of reducing welfare though the profit attained by the firm is larger. Referring to Fig.3.2 it may be noted that A is the welfare attainable if there is external pressure whereas the lack of external pressure reduces it to B primarily due to excessive cost[21].

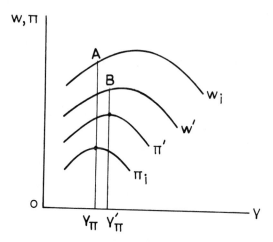

Figure 3.2. Costs and Welfare

The absence of internal pressure adds to inefficiency as illustrated in Fig.3.3. It may therefore be argued that the lack of internal and/or external pressure increases costs above the minimum possible for the organizational design under consideration. The observed level of welfare will not be the maximum attainable even if some increase over that which is expected under the market mode is discernible[22].

In conclusion, a welfare analysis of nonprice competition and internal decisions of the firm can be summed up in the form of three propositions.

---

[21] Let I^* denote the level of I preferred by the consumers. The demand curve $p(Y, I^*)$ is then relevant for drawing the W_i curve. The concept of the lack of external pressure would become relevant only if
  (a) the consumer valuation $p(Y)$ is normally independent of I, or
  (b) the I^* defined earlier exists
[22] It should be noted that though W' is below W_i it would nevertheless remain above W_m. For, otherwise, the internalization process will not be profitable from the viewpoint of the firm as well. Equivalently, referring to Fig.3.2, the acutal costs for a level A of Y will never be equal to or greater than C. For, if the inefficiency reaches such a level the firm would benefit by returning to the market mode.

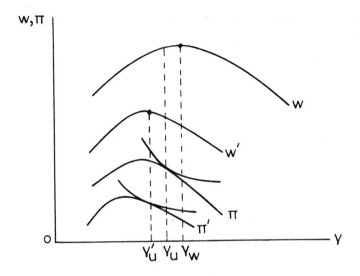

Figure 3.3. Internal Pressure and Efficiency

(a) There cannot be any organizational inefficiency so long as the firm has the internal pressure to maximize profits and internal decisions do not have the effect of reducing external pressure.

(b) So long as an internal decision has the effect of reducing external pressure there will be inefficiency even if the firm is a profit maximizer.

(c) The absence of internal pressure can, in general, create inefficiency. For, if the objective of maximum profits is not pursued then the costs can eventually catch up with any increase in prices that may be obtained due to lack of external pressure.

Whether the lack of internal and/or external pressure emerges in a specific organizational context, given the nature of the product market, remains an empirical question.

3.4. A BASIC MODEL

The primary motivation for internalization is the cost reduction which results from

(a) the production interdependence and external economies within teams described by Alchian and Demsetz (1972),

(b) the economies of scope and sharing of fixed inputs noted by Penrose (1959) and Baumol et al. (1982), and/or

(c) the saving of transaction costs as originated by Coase (1937).

Only the first two features of the cost function will be considered in the present chapter. Hence, to keep the presentation simple, it will be assumed that the market for the internalized input is competitive. That is, a unit of the input can also be purchased on the market at a fixed price q per unit. Note that q = marginal cost of producing the unit of input if it is produced by another firm. Let $C^*(Y, I)$ be the cost curve of the firm after it internalizes production of I. Let C_1^* and C_2^* denote the partial derivatives of C^* with respect to Y and I respectively. Clearly, $C_2^* > 0$, $C_{12}^* < 0$ for small values of I due to the existence of economies of scope. However, in the initial stages of input production, where capacity is not yet exhausted, it can be expected that $C_2^* < q$. Hence, the net marginal cost of internalizing an additional unit of I is negative. Let

$$C(Y, I) = C^*(Y, I) - qI$$

denote the net cost to the firm of producing Y. It follows that

$$C_2 = C_2^* - q < 0$$

for small values of I. It is this net cost advantage in the presence of economies of scope which provides the firm the basic motivation to internalize[23] the production of I. Evidently, $C_2 > 0$ for relatively large values of I. Both $C_{12} = C_{12}^* < 0$ and $C_2 < 0$ are essential in the rest of the analysis.

Nonprice competition shifts the demand curves whether or not it has an effect on the costs of production and sale of the final output. Since the information contained in nonprice signals can be evaluated by the consumers it will be presumed that there is a finite limit on the shifts in the demand curve.

Referring to Fig.3.4(a), let D be the demand curve for the final product, MC_m the marginal cost that can be attained after internalization. Similarly, let D_n be the ceiling demand curve under nonprice competition as in Fig.3.4(b). The shaded areas denote the maximum expected increase in welfare. Clearly, a combination of both these situations may arise in practice. The efficiency question, in the context of internal organization, pertains to the achievement of these maximum welfare gains that are conceptually possible.

Note that in the first case the welfare fuction can be written as

$$W = \int_0^Y p(y)dy - C(Y, I)$$

---

[23] There are several circumstance in which a market cannot exist and/or function in a viable manner. The following examples are typical of such situations:

    (a) Bates and Parkinson (1982, pp. 299ff) pointed out that inadequate demand for inputs and components, in the early stages of the product life cycle, may make an independent market for inputs nonoperational.

    (b) In the process of dynamic evolution of a firm it may develop specific assets such as new product designs, new marketing abilities and new technologies. And yet they may not be able to market these without jeopardizing the opportunities of the existing product lines. The only alternative for the firm in such cases may be to internalize production.

    (c) The Coase argument of Fig.3.1 indicates that transaction costs may make market operation less efficient.

    (d) Carlton (1979) pointed out that internalization may be due to the need to reduce the risks of input supply in monopolistic markets.

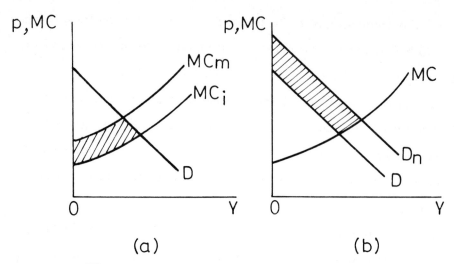

Figure 3.4. Internalization and External Pressure

where W = welfare, $p(Y)$ = price per unit of Y, Y = output of the firm, I = level of input production within the firm, and $C(Y, I)$ = cost of producing a given Y and I. The internal organization would then be efficient if, for a given Y, I is chosen to minimize $C(Y, I)$. Similarly, in the second case, W becomes

$$W = \int_0^Y p[y, I^*(y)]dy - C(Y, I)$$

where $I^*(Y)$ represents the consumer valuation of the nonprice dimension. Once again, welfare maximum requires that I should satisfy $C_2(Y, I) = 0$. Hence, for all practical purposes, the internal organization of the firm can be said to be efficient if I is chosen to minimize $C(Y, I)$ for any given Y.

The incentive mechanisms within the organization may not be strictly related to profit sharing by the managers. Whether or not profit maximization and cost minimization will be necessarily pursued cannot be determined apriori. Suppose the product market is competitive. Then competition eliminates profits in the long run and consequently generates internal pressure to minimize costs even for such organizational forms. For, otherwise survival is threatened. However, it cannot be claimed that imperfect product markets will be necessarily characterized by a lack of internal pressure. Stated differently, internal pressure or the lack of it is related to the incentive mechanisms within organizations rather than the market structure.

The lack of internal pressure will be represented by

$$U = \text{utility of the management} = U(\pi, I)$$

where π is the level of profits for the firm. In general, it may be argued that the rewards to the managers depend partly on the profit sharing incentive schemes within the firm and as a result $U_1 > 0$. Hence, generating a certain minimum profit is one of the properties of U. In one version the managers have been hypothesized to maximize such things as the rate of growth of the firm, sales or its rate of growth, or the size of the firm. For, the benefits to management from integration and increased size of the firm can be

(a) a reduction in anxiety regarding the regularity of the supply and the quality of input, and

(b) security of job and greater scope for exercising their powers.

In such a case $U_2 > 0$. The second alternative considers the possibility that, within the bounds of survival, the managers will regard the integration and expansion of the firm as creating a personal cost. The disutility of effort involved in cost reduction policies and expansion may be considered as being disproportionate to the expected share of profits. In such a case the manager may tradeoff certain profits in order to reduce the disutility of managerial effort. U_2 will then be negative. In either case, the magnitude of U_2 depends on a number of factors.

(a) U_2 will be small if the incentive mechanisms within the organization contain profit sharing clauses.

(b) The manager would be compelled to reduce the disutility of increases in I if changes in I have a significant impact on π and the market is not allowing any slack.

(c) The manager would place a high valuation on the disutility of effort if it has a negligible influence on π.

The firm can be considered as experiencing external pressure so long as the expected market price, for a given quantity of output, is parametric whatever the market environment may be. Hence, the influence of the internal decision process of the firm will have to be viewed as a fundamental specification of the lack of external pressure.

3.5. CONDITIONS FOR ORGANIZATIONAL EFFICIENCY

The basic result of this section is that the presence of both internal and external pressure would be sufficient to ensure organizational efficiency. The existence of external pressure implies that the demand curve can be represented by $p = p(Y)$. Similarly, the firm is a profit maximizer since it is assumed to experience internal pressure.

The decisions of the firm with respect to Y and I satisfy the equations

$$p[1 - (\frac{1}{\eta})] - C_1 = 0, \tag{1}$$

$$C_2 = 0 \tag{2}$$

where η is the elasticity of demand, and the usual second order conditions.

From this it is evident that, for a given Y, the firm will choose I so as to minimize the total cost of production

The nature of the equilibrium values of (Y, I) is represented in Fig.3.5 where E_1 and E_2 are the trajectories of equations (1) and (2) respectively. Further, E_1 will be steeper than E_2 due to the second order conditions. The relationship between the equilibrium choice of I and economies of scope depends on the market conditions for the output Y.

The following example will be useful. Let

$$p = p(Y) = 2\alpha - \beta Y,$$
$$C = C(Y, I) = F + aY^2 + bI^2 - 2mYI.$$

The profit maximizing choices of Y and I satisfy the equations

$$\alpha - (a + \beta) + mI = 0, \quad \text{and}$$
$$-bI + mY = 0.$$

Clearly, the choice of I, for the Y chosen, minimizes the cost of production.

It can now be verified that the choice of I, for the Y chosen by the firm, is independent of the elasticity of demand and always satisfies the condition $C_2(Y, I) = 0$ under the present assumptions. This result holds despite the change in the equilibrium values of Y and I since both the choices are still along the trajectory $C_2(Y, I) = 0$. This confirms the claim made earlier that the nature of the product market, as reflected by the elasicity of demand, is irrelevant in evaluating the efficiency in the choice of I.

3.6. EMERGENCE OF INEFFICIENCY

The impact of the lack of external pressure on the efficiency of in-

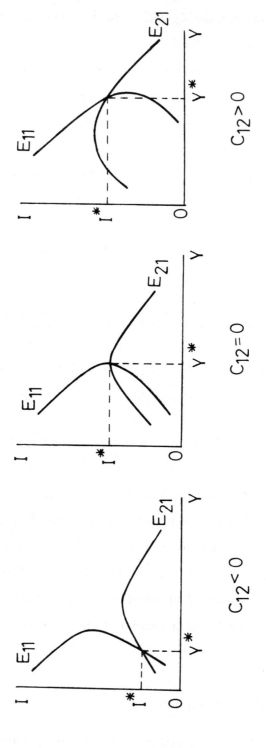

Figure 3.5. Equilibrium Values of Y and I

ternal organization may now be explored. Recall that the lack of external pressure will be characterized by

$$p = p(Y, I); \quad p_2 > 0.$$

The conditions for profit maximization are

$$p[1 - (\frac{1}{\eta})] - C_1 = 0,$$
$$p_2 Y - C_2 = 0 \tag{3}$$

and the appropriate second order conditions. Equation (3) indicates that the choice of I is such that $C_2 = p_2 Y > 0$. Hence, in the absence of external pressure, the level of I will be chosen in such a way that the cost to the firm, of producing the optimal Y, will be greater than the minimum necessary. The internal organization of the firm will be inefficient.

The efficient level of the internal decision, for the Y chosen to maximize π, is represented in Fig.3.6 by I^*. However, due to the lack of external pressure, the total profit of the firm is maximized at I'. The amount of excessive cost is given by the area FI^*I'.

Referring to the example of the previous section, let the demand curve change to

$$p = 2\alpha - \beta Y + 2\gamma I; \quad \gamma > 0.$$

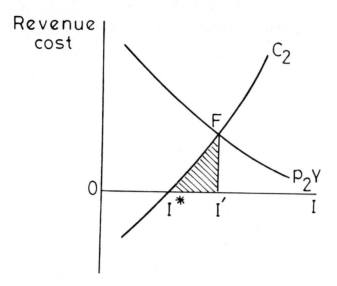

Figure 3.6. Inefficiency Due to Lack of External Pressure

Then the profit maximizing Y and I satisfy the equations

$$\alpha - (a + \beta)Y + (m + \gamma)I = 0, \quad \text{and}$$

$$(m + \gamma)Y - bI = 0.$$

Thus, though there is an increase in both Y and I, the choice of I is inefficient.

Lack of internal pressure can by itself, be a source of inefficiency. Assume, to begin with, that the firm experiences external pressure. Recall that the lack of internal pressure can be represented by

$$U = U(\pi, I) = U^*(Y, I).$$

The utility maximizing choices of Y and I satisfy the equations

$$p[1 - (\frac{1}{\eta})] - C_1 = 0, \quad \text{and}$$
$$U_2 - U_1 C_1 = 0 \tag{4}$$

along with the second order conditions. Hence, it can be concluded that, due to the lack of internal pressure, the firm does not choose an I in such a way as to minimize the total costs of production for the Y it produces. Hence, the choice of I is inefficient. The ratio U_2/U_1 can be looked upon as a measure of inefficiency. Fig.3.7 is drawn to illustrate the

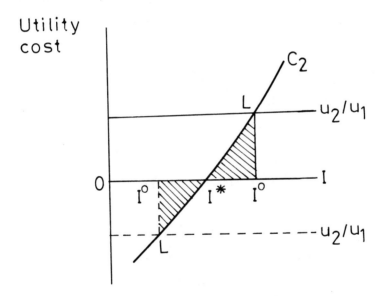

Figure 3.7. Inefficiency Due to Lack of Internal Pressure

cost increase due to inefficient choice of I. The utility maximizing choice creates an additional cost represented by the area $I^* I^O L$.

Reconsider the example cited earlier. Let the utility function of the manager be

$$U(\pi, I) = s\pi + 2vI.$$

Then, the utility maximizing choices of Y and I are such as to satisfy the equations

$$\alpha - (a + \beta)Y + mI = 0, \quad \text{and}$$
$$s(-bI + mY) + v = 0.$$

It can be readily verified that

$$C_2 = 2(bI - mY) = 2v/s$$

and that the cost of producing the Y chosen by the firm is not minimized.

It will now be shown that the simultaneous effect of the lack of internal and external pressures on the choices of I would have an additive effect on inefficiency. For, in this case, the first order conditions for utility maximization can be written as

$$p[1 - (\frac{1}{\eta})] - C_1 = 0, \quad \text{and}$$
$$C_2 = (U_2/U_1) + p_2Y \tag{5}$$

Referring to Fig.3.8 it can be inferred that $I^*I'F$ is the cost increase due to the lack of external pressure while an additional cost $FI'I_0T$ results from the lack of internal pressure. A similar result holds even in the case where $U_2 < 0$ because the inefficiency cannot be eliminated except by a coincidence.

3.7. CONCLUSION

The existence of economies of scope, whether they are technological or organization related, has been one of the factors responsible for the emergence of internal organization. However, there have been some doubts about such organizational modes sustaining the minimum possible cost. Market related properties, such as the elasticity of demand and the reduction in the number of firms due to possible barriers to entry, are insufficient to explain the emergence of inefficiency in such internal organizational modes. It has been demonstrated in this chapter that two features, intrinsic to the organization and incentive mechanisms contained within it, described as the lack of internal and external pressure, are responsible for inefficiency. Analysis of the welfare effects of organizational structures as well as nonprice competition can be systematized on this basis.

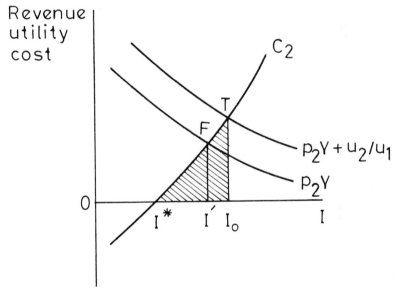

Figure 3.8. Overall Inefficiency

It can generally be expected that the mixed mode of organization becomes viable only if there is some cost reduction in contrast to the purely market mode. However, the welfare gains may not be the maximum that can be expected. This is the only notion of inefficiency which

CHAPTER 4

QUALITY OF PRODUCTS

4.1. THE ISSUES

The central theme of Chamberlin's monopolistic competition is that firms would generally find product differentiation as a preferable alternative to price competition. By appropriately choosing the quality (or variety) of products offered on the market they can generate a market advantage for themselves.

The characterization of quality has itself been subject to various interpretations. For, generally the quality of a product can be looked upon as any measurable characteristic of a commodity which has a value to the consumer. Several interpretations have been adopted in the literature. Chief among them are

(a) the durability of a commodity as measured by its economic life,

(b) the quality of service, such as the level of comfort in different modes of transportation, or any other characteristic which distinguishes it from substitutable products, and

(c) reliability of service as measured by the failure rates and costs of maintenance.

However, there can be many other aspects which make the quality of the product of a firm different from that of another firm[24].

In practice the consumer pays a price for each unit of the commodity purchased and the valuation of the embodied quality, if any, remains implicit. In some cases, where the equipment is rented and payments are

---

[24] Advertising by a firm may also be considered as a dimension of product differentiation and as a quality measure. This will be considered explicitly in the next chapter.

for the services rendered alone, there is a possibility that the consumer does not have any explicit preference for the quality or durability of the equipment itself. Similarly, as Cheung (1983, pp. 8-9) pointed out, the consumers cannot evaluate the functions of specific components of the commodity and as such cannot express a preference for their quality. From an analytical point of view the following alternatives are possible:

(a) the consumer pays for the services alone and has no preference for quality beyond the services provided,

(b) the consumer cannot and does not express preferences for quality but instead accepts whatever quality is available on the market, or

(c) the consumer has an explicit preference for quality and evaluates market price in such a context.

Whenever interpretation (c) is adopted the absence of a separate price valuation for the quality of the product has been a major source of the analytical problems in defining an economically efficient level of quality choices of firms.

The reactions of rival firms, to the variations in quality of products introduced by any one firm in the market, can themselves be quite diverse. For a monopolistic firm may find it far more difficult and expensive to obtain the information regarding quality differences of rivals as compared to the information about their prices. Under these conditions firms may prefer to maintain a higher quality and shift demand curves in their favor rather than indulge in price competition for a given quality. In other words, lack of external pressure and the ability of firms to charge prices disproportionate to quality variations are more likely under conditions of monopolistic competition. That is, as Leibenstein (1980, pp. 228-9) claims, the firms would prefer to create a shelter from the market through non-market characteristics rather than alter the market price of output.

Assume, for purposes of argument, that the management of the firm is aware of the implicit quality valuation of the consumer even if the market demand curve does not reflect it explicitly. Then, in its attempt to accommodate such choices, the firm will experience an increase in marginal cost. Given this property of the cost curves and the preferences of the management for nonmarket shelter, a firm which tries to cater to the implicit quality choice of the consumer may experience costs of production which are not minimal. Based on the traditional definition of economic efficiency the possibility of an inefficient choice arising from the cost side of the decision process cannot be ruled out.

The foregoing analysis indicates that the economic efficiency of the quality choice of a firm depends upon

(a) the nature of the product market,

(b) the explicit cost minimization by the management, and

(c) the identification and explicit use of the implicit information regarding the consumer's quality choice as a function of the level of output.

The primary purpose of the present chapter is to examine these aspects in some detail in an endeavor to arrive at an operational definition of the economic efficiency of quality choice.

4.2. DURABILITY OF PRODUCTS

Neoclassical welfare economics, which does not explicitly deal with the quality of products, defines the level of output (Y) chosen by a firm to be economically efficient if and only if

$$p(Y) = \text{price per unit of } Y$$

$$= MC(Y)$$

$$= \text{marginal cost of producing a unit of } Y.$$

This definition presumes that

(a) the consumer can obtain the relevant information about the price of the commodity without any transaction (search) costs, and

(b) the firm minimizes the cost of producing Y.

The actual output choice of the firm is considered to be inefficient if this equation is not satisfied. The primary source of allocative inefficiency is the nature of the market and the extent of the inelasticity of demand for the product of the firm.

Most of the recent literature on the quality choice of firms does not contain an explicit definition of the efficient quality level. Instead, they compare the quality choice of profit maximizing firms operating in different markets. However, even if this conceptualization is regarded as adequate, there is no consensus on the direction of change implied by different market structures. In particular, Levhari and Srinivasan (1969) argued that the quality of monopoly goods would be lower. On the other hand, Dreze and Hagen (1978), along with several others, demonstrated that it can be higher. It is also well known that Swan (1970) and Sieper and Swan (1973) hold the view that the quality choice is not affected by the nature of the market.

A few of these results can be restructured in the welfare maximizing framework to examine the inefficiency of the quality choice in different markets and its sources. Following Levhari and Srinivasan (1969) let each unit of the durable good in existence provide one unit of flow services to the consumer. Let S be the stock of serviceable durables in existence[25] at the beginning of a time period and F be the flow services demanded by the consumer during a given interval of time. Then the flow purchases of the durable would be

$$Y = F - S.$$

Let the price which the consumer is willing to pay for a unit of flow services be[26]

$$p = p(S + Y); \quad p_1 < 0$$

where $p_1 = dp(S+Y)/d(S+Y)$. Assume, to being with, that the services of a durable can be obtained only if the durable is purchased and owned. Then, following Levhari and Srinivasan, the price per unit of Y can be written as

$$p^*(Y) = p(S + Y)g(Q), \quad \text{where}$$
$$g(Q) = (1 - e^{-rQ})/r, \quad \text{and}$$

$r = $ rate of discount per unit of time[27]. Assume that the cost of production can be expressed as

$$TC(Y) = aYC(Q).$$

---

[25] The durability of this stock at the beginning is not relevant for the determination of the quality choice at any point of time. The discerning reader would have noted the difference in this assumption from that of Levhari and Srinivasan. Naturally some of the results in the sequel are different.

[26] This is the assumption in Levhari and Srinivasan (1969). In general, the possibility that p depends on Q is not considered to be plausible. This is an acceptable assumption so long as the quality of flow services is not a function of durability.

[27] Note that $g(Q)$ is not a specification of the preferences of the consumers. Instead, it is merely a discounting formula.

Further, let $C(Q)$ be convex. That is,

$$C_1^2 - CC_{11} > 0.$$

The essential problem is one of defining the efficient level of Q. Consider

$$W(Y, Q) = \text{total welfare}$$
$$= g(Q) \int_0^Y p(S + y)dy - aYC(Q).$$

Then, the first order conditions for the maximum of $W(Y, Q)$ with respect to Y and Q are respectively

$$g(Q)p(S + Y) - aC(Q) = 0, \quad \text{and}$$
$$[\int_0^Y p(S + y)dy]g_1(Q) - aYC_1(Q) = 0.$$

Recall from Spence (1977) that

$$\int_0^Y p(S + y)dy = Yp(S + Y)/[1 - (\frac{1}{\eta})]$$

where η is the elasticity of demand. Hence, it follows that

$$C_1(Q)/C(Q) = g_1(Q)/[g(Q)\{1 - (\frac{1}{\eta})\}].$$

The economically efficient choice of Q must satisfy this equation.

Consider the profit maximizing choice of Y and Q. Recalling that

$$\pi = Yp(S + Y)g(Q) - C(Q)$$

it can be verified that

$$\frac{\partial \pi}{\partial Y} = 0 = p[1 - (\frac{1}{\eta})]g(Q) - aC(Q)$$

$$\frac{\partial \pi}{\partial Q} = 0 = Ypg_1(Q) - aYC_1.$$

Hence, it follows that the welfare maximizing Q will be obtained in the context of profit maximizing firms irrespective of the markets in which they operate. In fact, the output quality, as defined by the above equation, is independent of the market price of Y. Hence, the choice of Q always remains economically efficient[28].

Referring again to Chapter 3 it should be reiterated that so long as the management experiences both external and internal pressure the choice of the quality would be economically efficient. The market structure has no bearing on this result. The monopolistic market creates an allocative inefficiency in the choice of Y alone[29].

However, as remarked in Section 5.1, managerial motivations may be such as to tradeoff a certain amount of profit to create an inelasticity of demand in the long run. Let the preference function of the management be

$$u = u(\pi, Q); \quad u_1 > 0, \quad u_2 > 0.$$

[28] The Q chosen by a monopoly firm may be less than that of a competitive firm. Thus, while the result of Levhari and Srinivasan is correct it does not indicate any inefficiency or welfare loss given their assumptions.
[29] This is a disadvantage of the constant marginal cost assumptions. For, in general, the allocative inefficiency in the choice of Y has implications for the choice of Q beyond those reflected in the elasticity of demand. This will be clear from the subsequent analysis.

Then, it follows that the choice of Y and Q would be such that

$$\frac{\partial u}{\partial Y} = u_1 \frac{\partial \pi}{\partial Y} = 0, \quad \text{and}$$

$$\frac{\partial u}{\partial Q} = u_1 \frac{\partial \pi}{\partial Q} + u_2 = 0$$

so that the Q choice will no longer satisfy the earlier equation. Hence, it can be concluded that the lack of internal pressure is one of the sources of managerial inefficiency in the choice of Q.

Similarly, the emergence of the lack of external pressure, as indicated by an inadequate response of rivals, can be shown to lead to an inefficient choice of Q. For, let

$$p = p(S + Y, Q)$$

be the demand curve for the flow services. Then, even if the firm maximizes profits, the choice of Y would be such that

$$p[1 - (\frac{1}{\eta})]g(Q) = aC(Q)$$

and the choice of Q satisfies the equation

$$p_2 g(Q) + p g_1(Q) = aC_1(Q)$$

so that the quality offered by the firm would no longer be economically efficient.

It should be obvious from the foregoing analysis that the inefficiency in the quality choice is compounded when both the pressures are absent.

Sieper and Swan (1973, p. 345) contend that an analysis of this nature is inapplicable when the firm leases the product to the consumers. However, it can be shown that the welfare argument is still valid. For, in such a case, if R is the rental charged by the firm per unit of time, the present discounted value of the stream of rentals would be $Rg(Q)$ and in a long run equilibrium this would be sufficient to cover the costs of production. That is,

$$g(Q) = aYC(Q)$$

so that the rental R per unit of time will be

$$R = \frac{aYC(Q)}{g(Q)}.$$

However, the demand for flow services will, as before, be

$$p = p(S + Y).$$

Hence, the welfare function can be written as

$$W(Y, Q) = \int_0^Y p(S + y)dy - aY[\frac{C(Q)}{g(Q)}].$$

Thus, as Sieper and Swan (1973, p. 339) observed, the choice of the level of durability is simply a question of cost minimization and the efficient choice is unrelated to the nature of the product market since $C(Q)/g(Q)$ is independent of Y.

From the present perspective it is important to note that the profit maximizing choice of Q also minimizes $C(Q)/g(Q)$ so that the existence of both external and internal pressure ensures an efficient choice of the quality of products. Further, it can be readily inferred that the absence of external and/or internal pressure leads to an inefficient quality choice.

4.3. Ex Post Demand as Standard

It is often acknowledged that the market for most of the commodities offers a rather wide variety of qualities for every level of output which the consumer chooses. It is therefore possible to assume that there is a large variety of goods which are substitutable in the provision of flow services. Seshinski (1976) and Leland (1977) postulated that the price per unit of Y of quality Q can be written as $p(Y, Q)$. This specification implies that given the price per unit of Y, the consumer is indifferent between a variety of combinations of Y and Q.

Essentially, given the choice of quality Q by the firm the consumer chooses a quantity Y such that

$$p = p(Y, Q); \quad p_1 < 0, \quad p_2 > 0.$$

This can be designated as the expost demand curve. Notice, however, that a welfare maximizing choice of Q can be defined.

Let the cost function for the firm be represented as

$$C = C(Y, Q).$$

The welfare function can be written as

$$W(Y, Q) = \int_0^Y p(y, Q)dy - C(Y, Q)$$

so that the welfare maximizing Y and Q satisfy the equations

$$p(Y, Q) = C_1(Y, Q),$$
$$\int_0^Y p_2(y, Q)dy = C_2(Y, Q).$$

On the other hand, the profit function for the firm will be

$$\pi(Y, Q) = Yp(Y, Q) - C(Y, Q).$$

The profit maximizing Y and Q are given by

$$p(Y,Q)[1 - (\frac{1}{\eta})] = C_1(Y,Q)$$
$$Y p_2(Y,Q) = C_2(Y,Q).$$

A comparison between this choice of Q and the welfare maximizing level can be set up by examining the extent to which the firm can convert the increases in welfare from better quality into revenues. Recall that from Spence (1977)

$$[1 - (\frac{1}{\eta})] \int_0^Y p(y,Q)dy = Y p(Y,Q).$$

Differentiating both sides with respect to Q it can be readily verified that

$$Y p_2 = [1 - (\frac{1}{\eta})] \int_0^Y p_2(y,Q)dy.$$

It is therefore obvious that, given a Y, the profit maximizing choice of Q also maximizes welfare. As before the presence of both external and internal pressure ensures welfare maximization in the quality choice. The differences, if any, are purely due to allocative inefficiency[30]. The nature of the product market imperfection is irrelevant for determining the efficiency in the choice of Q.

It is rather elementary to verify that the absence of external and/or internal pressure induces inefficient quality choice.

---

[30] Most of the literature dealing with non-price competition accepts the expost demand curves as the welfare standard. Since market imperfection creates changes in Y and correspondingly some changes in Q they are being considered as inefficiency explained by the inealsticity of demand, number of firms, barriers to entry etc. It should be evident from the present analysis that inefficiencies in the choice of Q can be more pervasive than those explained by market characteristics alone.

4.4. Demand for Quality

The availablity of a wide range of choices may induce the consumer to search for a quantity and quality combination. Miller (1961) and Parks (1974) noted that there can be transaction (search, information) costs. Confronted by these costs the consumer may then stop searching for a better quality if the transaction costs exceed the marginal valuation. Similarly, Parks (1974) has also shown that there may be an increased operating cost associated with products of higher quality. Even this tends to limit the quality level which the consumer chooses. However, notice that the consumer preference for intrinsic quality is not captured by this formulation. For, if two consumers differ in their choice of quality it is primarily due to search costs.

Consequently, it has been difficult to assess the role of quality choice of the consumer in the observed demand curve for output. In general, the characterization of the choice of Q, implicitly as a function of the level of output, has been missing. However, Seshinski (1976, p. 131) pointed out that the quantity and quality may be substitutable in the sense that a consumer who buys a small quantity tends to prefer a higher quality. Further, the analysis of Irish (1980) indicates that the quality choice for a given Y may depend on the market price for the output.

Hence, as Sweeny (1974, p. 140) contends, "any definition of quality that is meaningful for consumer choice theory must be based upon a notion of consumer preferences for one commodity over a substitute commodity." The consumer has a valuation of Y independently of, or as a function of the market price of Y. The choices of Y and Q must be specified as a simultaneous decision process. However, the most difficult conceptual problem in developing a general result is the identification of a proper specification of the choice of quality by consumers.

To begin with assume that the market for the commodity offers a rather wide variety of qualities for every level of output which the consumer chooses. There will be a choice of Q for every output level Y chosen. Secondly, it will be postulated that the consumer views the services obtained from Y units of output of quality Q to be $y(Y, Q)$. However, it is well-known that $y(Y, Q)$ may exhibit both substitution and complementarity relationships. For, there will be some consumers who place a high valuation on Q at low values of Y and conversely. But it is conceivable that for the same commodity there will be other consumers who are far more particular about quality when they buy a large amount of Y than they would if Y were smaller. These properties of quality choice have been noted by Seshinski (1976).

If there is a substitution relationship it follows that for any given Y there exists a $Q = q(Y)$ which maximizes the satisfaction derived from the given Y. Even when Y and Q are complementary it is conceivable that there is a limit on Q for a given Y. The primary reason would then be the transaction and operating cost considerations alluded to by Parks (1974). For the present purposes it will be assumed that the limit $Q = q(Y)$ exists. However, q_1 may be positive or negative[31].

With these notions in perspective the demand curve for Y can be developed in the following manner[32]. Let X represent a composite commodity in the budget of the consumer. Assume for simplicity that the price per unit of X is unity. Postulate the existence of a well-defined utility function $u^*[X, y(Y, Q)]$. Then, the problem for the consumer is to

---

[31] When Q and Y are complementary, it may be expected that the price per unit of Y and the total expenditure would define $Q = q(Y, p)$. The dependence of quality choice on the price per unit of Y is unlikely in the case of substitutes.

[32] The studies of Seshinski (1976) as well as Dreze and Hagen (1978) start with similar premises though they deviate away when consumer choice is considered explicitly.

choose X, Y and Q so as to maximize $u^*[X, y(Y, Q)]$ subject to

$$X + pY = I$$

where $I =$ income of the consumer. In general, the choices satisfy the budget constraint along with

$$u_1^* - \lambda = 0$$

$$u_2^* y - \lambda p = 0, \quad \text{and}$$

$$u_2^* y_2 = 0$$

where λ is a Lagrange multiplier. If there are transaction costs and/or operating costs associated with an increase in quantity, the last equation can be written as $u_2^* y_2 = \beta$ where $\beta =$ cost per unit of Q. In either case it can be shown that the demand curves take the form

$$p = p[Y, q(Y)]$$

where $q(Y)$ is, in general, obtained by solving the equation[33]

$$u_2^* y_2 = \beta.$$

Such a demand curve satisfies the following conditions:

$$p_1 < 0, \quad p_2 > 0, \quad \frac{dp}{dY} < 0.$$

---

[33] That is, given a price p per unit of Y, there is a specific choice of Y and a corresponding choice of $q(Y)$. From this it may be noted that the quality choice may depend on β, the transaction or operating cost, as well as the price p per unit of Y. In such a case the demand curves should be written as $Y = Y(p)$, and $Q = Q(p, \beta)$ given income I. This would be similar to the specification of Irish (1980). However, if $\beta = 0$ the choice of $q(Y)$ is such that $y(Y, Q)$ is maximized and is independent of the price p per unit of Y. In either case, the results of the following section would be valid except for minor changes in algebra.

However, as has already been pointed out, dp/dY can be positive as well.

Notice that, in this formulation, a given Y spans a preference for Q. But, unlike the Leland (1977) framework, the preference originates with the consumer. Secondly, a market will determine the economically efficient Y and consequently an efficient Q. The spanning approach is once again useful. But the present formulation is fundamentally different from that of Leland (1977) as well as Murphy (1980).

This is the basic result needed for developing the concept of the economically efficient choice of quality.

4.5. QUALITY PREFERENCE AND EFFICIENCY

In order to reduce the analysis to the minimum essentials consider a firm which has a market demand curve

$$p = p(Y, Q), \quad \text{and}$$
$$Q = q(Y).$$

Let the costs of production be represented by

$$C = C(Y, Q).$$

The economically efficient choices of Y and Q then maximize the welfare function

$$W(Y, Q) = \int_0^Y p[x, q(Y)]dx - C(Y, Q).$$

It follows from this that, for any given Y, the quality level Q which minimizes $C(Y, Q)$ is economically efficient. Dreze and Hagen (1978, p. 505) noted this result. For, it was pointed out that if the demand curves were invariant with respect to the variations in Q, each of the firms would have to choose a quality level which minimizes the cost of production.

In general, the marginal costs of increasing Q will be positive and increasing. Hence, the cost minimization concept has yet to be concretely defined. Two approaches to the problem are available. Rewrite the cost function in the form

$$C(Y, Q) = C[Y, q(Y)] + [Q - q(Y)]C_2$$

where C_2 is the marginal cost of Q. Since $C_2, C_{22} > 0$, the minimum value of $C(Y, Q)$, subject to $Q \geq q(Y)$, is attained when $Q = q(Y)$. This is the efficient choice of Q. A somewhat better insight into the welfare maximization process can be attained in the following manner. Let the welfare function be rewritten as

$$W(Y, Q) = \int_0^Y p(x, Q)dx - C(Y, Q).$$

Then, expanding $p(x, Q)$ around $Q = 0$, it follows that

$$p(x, Q) = p(x) + Qp_2(x)$$

so that

$$\int_0^Y p(x, Q)dx = \int_0^Y p(x)dx + Q \int_0^Y p_2(x)dx.$$

Redefine the net social cost of providing a quality Q as

$$C'(Y, Q) = C(Y, Q) - Q \int_0^Y p_2(x)dx$$

when Q is small, the consumer preferences would indicate that the gains of increasing Q exceed costs. That is, $C_2' < 0$ upto $Q = q(Y)$. Beyond this Q the net social cost will begin to rise. Hence, the welfare maximum, which requires that the net social cost be minimized, results in the efficient choice of Q given by $Q = q(Y)$.

It can now be noted that, given a Y, the profit maximizing firm would also choose the economically efficient level of Q. Under conditions of monopolistic competition the inefficient choice of Y also leads to an inefficient choice of Q. However, to the extent that costs are minimum for a given Y this cannot be classified as managerial inefficiency. Stated differently, the choice of Q, for a given Y, remains economically efficient so long as the firm experiences both internal and external pressure.

As before, it can also be verified that the lack of external and/or internal pressure leads to an inefficient choice of Q. The primary reason for the inefficiency is that the firm does not pursue cost minimization under the new configuration.

Leland (1977, p. 135) argued that the inefficiency in the choice of Q is basically due to the inability of the firm to convert the increased consumer utility into revenue and thus cover costs. This is the market induced or allocative inefficiency. In addition, the choice of Q can be inefficient if the management

(a) does not maximize profits,

(b) inadequate rival reactions provide an effective shelter for the firm. Very often the inefficiency induced by managerial choices cannot be ignored even if it cannot be measured concretely.

In general, the market induced imperfection indicates that the actual quality chosen by the firms would be less than efficient. The other two sources indicate the opposite. It may be expected that when the two effects are taken together the quality choice would be greater than the economically efficient level. For, a monopolistic firm may find that the rivals can obtain information about prices far more easily compared to the information regarding their quality. Under these conditions, they would prefer to maintain a higher quality, rather than price competition given quality, so as to enable them to derive additional profits. Departures from efficiency and the consequent creation of monopoly power are more likely in those directions which cannot be easily detected from the market price alone.

4.6. CONCLUSION

It was noted at the outset that the quality of products in monopolistic competition can be defined in several ways. The concept of efficiency in the quality choice has been concretized in the context of the three major notions adopted in the literature. One of the major conclusions is that inefficiency in the quality choice can be due to

(a) market imperfection and the inefficient choice of Y,

(b) lack of external pressure on the management, and/or

(c) lack of internal pressure on the decision makers.

Consumer valuation of the quality of products can be incorporated explicitly whenever such preferences are likely to be observed. A proper respecification of the demand curves once again indicates that the above three propositions regarding inefficient quality choice are valid.

Dynamic considerations are essential in the context of the product differentiation strategies of monopolistic firms. To the extent that built-in obsolescence can reduce external pressure and keep the demand curve stable, the quality of products may be lower. Thus the net effect of the different sources of inefficiency remains an empirical question. However, from a theoretical viewpoint, the sources of inefficiency are clearly beyond those induced by market imperfection alone.

CHAPTER 5

SEARCH COSTS, ADVERTISING AND WELFARE

5.1. THE ISSUES

Advertising and selling costs, which are essential features of the product markets under monopolistic competition, have significant implications for welfare economics[34]. Three basic mechanisms, through which advertising affects welfare have been identified:

(a) the demand curve for the firm, which is altered due to the changes in the consumer preferences,

(b) the cost at which the product is made available to the consumer, and

(c) the strategies of rival firms in the market and their effect on the nature of the demand curve for a firm.

Chamberlin (1962, p. 279) noted that, as a result of the firms incurring a selling cost, the consumers may be getting something they do not want and may be precluded from obtaining what they do want. The possibility of the level of advertising being excessive in relation to the welfare maximum was examined in the literature in such a context.

Chamberlin did not examine consumer preferences adequately while considering the effect of advertising on the demand curve for a firm. However, there are four pertinent remarks:

(a) selling costs incurred by any one firm can alter the preferences of the consumers by providing them information about its product. See Chamberlin (1962, pp. 275ff),

---

[34] Much of the pertinent literature is reviewed in Comanor and Wilson (1979), Lambin (1976, Ch. 1), and Utton (1982, Ch. 4).

(b) the firm has to incur an increasing selling cost to entice the consumer to buy an additional unit of its product (p. 135),

(c) the actual level of advertising chosen by a firm will not necessarily be the one for which the demand is the greatest (p. 146), and

(d) "advertising outlay by any one seller gains customers from his rivals and alters the demand curves for their products." — p. 140.

Subsequent work of Nelson (1974), Nichols (1985) and others specified the consumer preference functions as either

(i) $u = u(X, Y, A)$, or

(ii) $u = u[X, Y(A)]$,

where X is the quantity of the composite commodity, Y is the quantity of an advertised good in the consumer budget, and A is the level of advertising by the firm. Such specifications generally imply a monotonically upward shift of the demand curve for Y with increases in the level of advertising. Attempts have been made to introduce the search costs of consumers into the analysis to provide concreteness to the remarks (b) and (c). For, the nature of monopolistic product market is such that the consumers will have to choose from a variety of differentiated products to satisfy a particular need. They require information about the characteristics of different products to make a choice. The collection of the requisite information entails some search costs. Advertising by the firms is an alternative to such search by the consumer. For, information, other than that based on the experience of using the product, can be obtained through advertising messages. Though Butters (1977), Wiggins and Lane (1983), Grossman and Shapiro (1984), and others made attempts to incorporate search costs into the analysis, it has not been possible to specify whether the consumer can and does express a preference for a certain level of advertising and thereby exhibit a ceiling demand curve[35]. One of the objectives of the present chapter is to give a concrete expression to this concept and examine its welfare implications.

Advertising also affects the costs of the firm. Hence, the changes in the marginal cost curves can also have an effect on welfare. However, most studies of advertising and welfare postulate constant marginal costs. See, for example, the often cited work of Dixit and Norman (1978, p. 6). Chamberlin (1962, p. 136ff), however, argued that the average cost curve will have the u-shape even when selling costs are added to the costs of production. This is more plausible since there is excess capacity under conditions of monopolistic competition. It should also be noted that consumer welfare is derived at a cost to the consumers in addition to the market price which they pay for the product. The total social costs comprising of

(a) the costs of production for the firm,

(b) the advertising and selling costs of the firm, and

(c) the search costs of the consumers

will have to be taken into account to provide an adequate definition of the welfare efficient level of advertising by the firm. This is the second objective of this study.

Analysis of the level of advertising chosen by the firms in monopolistic competition also suggests that it is excessive in relation to the welfare maximum. What are the sources of this inefficiency? The answer from the existing literature is that certain features of the product market are responsible for the inefficiency. In particular, the elasticity of demand, number of firms, and barriers to entry are cited. However, as Chamberlin (1962, pp. 284ff) and several subsequent studies pointed out, the relation-

---

[35] The question of inadequate response from rival firms and its implications for welfare will be considered in the sequel.

ship between the elasticity of demand and the number of firms or barriers to entry is not clear. Secondly, the effect of cost changes on consumer welfare has not been properly examined so far. For instance, the remark of Chamberlin (1962, p. 146) that the combined cost curve of the firm may not be the lowest has not been pursued in the analysis of welfare loss. One of the main problems has been the identification of the source of such cost increases if they occur. Thirdly, the changes in the demand curves, due to the reactions of the rival firms alluded to by Chamberlin (1962, p. 146), have not been accounted for. Fourthly, the behavioral theories of the firm indicated the possibility that the management of the firm may value size per se and maximize a preference function of the form $u(\pi, Y)$ or $u(\pi, A)$ rather than the profit itself. The implications of such preferences for costs of production and sales in addition to the changes in output will also have to be accounted for in studies of the level of advertising being excessive. This is the third objective of the present study.

In sum, it will be argued

(a) that changes in consumer demand and social costs implied by the presence of consumer search costs are essential mechanisms through which advertising affects welfare.

(b) that there is a necessity to redefine the efficient level of advertising taking the social costs as well as the ceiling demand curves into account, and

(c) that the major sources of inefficiency are intrinsic to the management of the strategy of nonprice competition. Such an analysis is necessary to obtain a comprehensive view of the effects of advertising and search costs on economic welfare.

5.2. Conventional Wisdom

It is well known that the profit (π) maximizing output (Y) choice of a monopolistic firm does not maximize W. The primary source of this inefficiency is the inelasticity of demand. For, as Spence (1977) noted, lower elasticity will not enable the firm to convert the consumer surplus into profits. The effect of advertising on the output choice, and its relation to the welfare maximizing levels of Y and A, has been examined by considering the changes in

(a) the elasticity of demand, and

(b) the position of the demand curve.

Further, it has been recognized that inefficiency in the choice of Y may be due to the product market conditions as well as an excessive level of advertising in comparison to the welfare maximizing quantity A. However, the deviation of the actual A from the welfare maximizing level has been attributed to market imperfection. Consequently, the changes in the demand curve alone have been emphasized even in this context. That is, deviations from welfare maximum have been attributed entirely to the product market characteristics.

Let A be the level of advertising currently chosen by the firm. Denote the demand curve for the firm by D_a and let MR be the corresponding marginal revenue curve. Then, as represented in Fig.5.1(a) the welfare maximizing level of output (Y_w) is always greater than the profit maximizing quantity (Y_π). Since this is valid for all levels of advertising chosen by the firm the welfare and profit maximizing levels of output can be represented by W and π in the (Y, A) plane. See Fig.5.1(b).

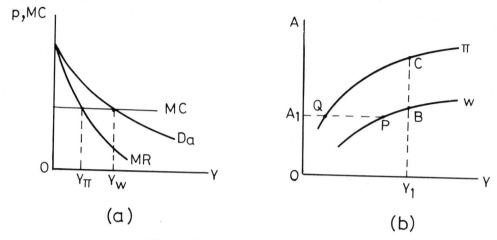

Figure 5.1. Profits and Welfare

Now, the traditional argument is that for a given level A_1 of advertising the firm would reduce output from P to Q and this is the source of welfare loss (allocative inefficiency). Inverting the argument, Dixit and Norman (1978) suggested that for a given level of output Y_1, the welfare maximizing level of advertising is B whereas the firm chooses C. This signals the possibility of excessive advertising. However, for a valid comparison, A_w corresponding to Y_w must be compared with A_π corresponding to Y_π. This is represented in Fig.5.2. It is evident from this figure that advertising may be excessive under certain conditions.

The following analytical approximation would be sufficient to highlight the existing results. Let the demand curve be represented by

$$p = \text{price per unit of } Y = p(Y, A), \quad \text{where}$$
$$p_1 = \frac{\partial p}{\partial Y} < 0, \quad \text{and} \quad p_2 = \frac{\partial p}{\partial A} > 0.$$

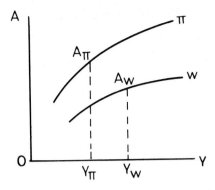

Figure 5.2. Excessive Advertising

Let

$$C = \text{total cost of production}$$

$$= C(Y, A) = c_1 Y + c_2 A$$

where c_1 and c_2 are assumed to be positive constants. Assuming that the post advertising level of the demand curve is relevant for welfare comparisons, let

$$W(Y, A) = \text{total surplus or welfare}$$

$$= \int_0^Y p(Y, A)dY - c_1 Y - c_2 A.$$

Consider the welfare maximizing choice of output (Y_w) and advertising (A_w). They satisfy the equations

$$p(Y, A) - c_1 = 0, \quad \text{and}$$

$$\int_0^Y p_2(y, A)dy - c_2 = 0$$

whereas the profit maximizing choice will be such that

$$p(Y, A)[1 - (\frac{1}{\eta})] - c_1 = 0, \quad \text{and}$$
$$Y p_2(Y, A) - c_2 = 0$$

where η is the elasticity of demand. Further,

$$Y p_2(Y, A) > \int_0^Y p_2(y, A) dy \quad \text{if} \quad p_{12} > 0$$

and the inequality wil be reversed whenever $p_{12} < 0$. Given this and the second order condition $p_{22} < 0$, Fig.5.3 is drawn to represent the choices

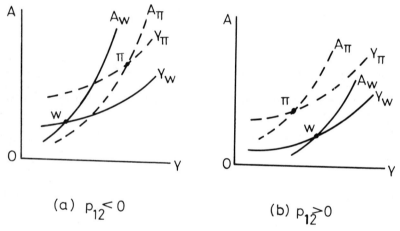

(a) $p_{12} \lessgtr 0$ (b) $p_{12} \gtrless 0$

Figure 5.3. Choices of Output and Advertising

of output and the level of advertising. In this diagram Y_w and A_w represent the trajectories of the first order conditions for welfare maximum. Similarly Y_π and A_π are the trajectories of the profit maximizing choices of Y and A. It can be readily verified that A_π is always to the left of A_w. However, the position of Y_π relative to Y_w depends on the sign of p_{12}. The two possible cases have been represented in Fig.5.3. From this it can be deduced that A_π at the equilibrium point π is almost always in excess of A_w at the point W. Hence, it can be generally argued that the market imperfection creates an inefficient choice of Y_π and this, in its turn, generates a choice of A_π in excess of A_w.

The following observations are pertinent:

(i) Referring to Fig.5.4(a), let W and π be the levels of welfare and profit at the pre-advertising level of demand. Then, if Fig.5.4(b) depicts the post advertising outcomes, the possibility that the welfare at E_a exceeds that at E cannot be ruled out. In other words, the inefficiency of advertising only refers to the maximum possible level of welfare not being attained in the post advertising configuration. It does not indicate that the post advertising level of welfare is reduced below that attained in the pre-advertising case.

(ii) Fig.5.4(c) represents a situation in which $A_\pi > A_w$, i.e., advertising is excessive. What is the relevant value of Y for drawing the W and π curves in this figure? Nichols (1985) utilizes Y_π throughout the analysis whereas Dixit and Norman (1978) consider the π curve for Y_π and the W curve for Y_w. The latter approach acknowledges that the allocative inefficiency in the choice of Y may, in itself, have some implications for the choice of the advertising level. However, the validity of welfare comparisons with the post advertising level of demand can be contested. For, a part of the observed shift in the demand curve for any one firm may be a result of an inadequate response from rival firms rather than being a reflection of consumer preferences[36].

It may be concluded that defining the consumer valuation of a given

---

[36] Suppose the advertising level is excessive. The preference functions adopted so far will still indicate an upward shift in the demand curve. This, in itself, creates difficulties in accepting the post advertising standard.

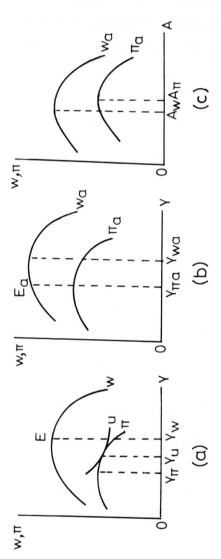

Figure 5.4. Post Advertising Level of Welfare

level of advertising, the corresponding ceiling demand curve, and its welfare implications are essential to an understanding of the level of advertising being excessive.

5.3. SEARCH COSTS

The consumer has to generally incur some search costs to collect the requisite information about differentiated products. The optimal amount of search depends upon a number of factors, including the number of firms in the market and product variety, the quantity of output purchased by the consumer and so on. The effect of advertising may be to provide a part of the information, reduce uncertainty regarding quality, and thereby reduce the search cost which the consumer has to incur in its absence.

Hence, the search cost of the consumers, per unit of output purchased, can be written as

$$s = s(A); \quad s_1 < 0, \quad s_{11} > 0$$

where s is the search cost per unit of output[37], and A is the level of advertising by the firm. Generally s_1 can be assumed to be negative since advertising is a substitute for the consumer search. However, s_{11} is expected to be positive since additional advertising by the firm provides a decreasing amount of information.

However, a firm which has a high level of advertising, via its effects on the costs of production and sales can have a tendency to increase the

---

[37] A more general specification of the search cost function would be to write $s(Y, A)$. However, it can be readily verified that there will be no essential change in the results of this study even when such a general specification is adopted. Hence, the simpler version will be used throughout.

price of its product. Let

$$p = p^* f(A) = \text{ price per unit of } Y.$$

The consumer compares this price with the reduction in search costs. Normally, the consumer would value A only to the extent that it reduces the total cost at which a unit of Y can be procurred for consumption. This, in its turn, is the sum of the market price and search cost. Hence, the choice of A would be optimal from the consumer viewpoint only if

$$p^* f_1(A) + s_1(A) = 0.$$

Let such a value of A be written as A'. The consumer would not be willing to pay for any advertising level beyond A' so defined. It follows from this that the consumer can and does express a preference for the level of advertising.

This first stage optimization suggests that one of the effects of advertising on the demand for Y is through the budget constraint of the consumer. To define this formally, let X be a composite commodity in the consumer budget. The consumer choice problem, in its simplest form, is to maximize $u^*(X, Y)$ subject to $[p^* f(A')]Y + X = I$ where u is the preference function, and I is the level of income.

The resulting choice of the quantity of Y demanded can therefore be written as

$$Y = Y(p, A')$$

or, the demand function becomes

$$p = p(Y, A'); \quad p_1 < 0, \quad p_2 > 0.$$

Following the analysis of Dixit and Norman (1978), Kotowitz and Math-ewson (1979) and others the preference function may also be modified to account for the effects of advertising. However, the basic nature of the demand curve is adequately reflected by the above formulation.

The following reinterpretation of the choice of A' would be helpful in subsequent analysis. Since the total expenditure of the consumer, on this variety of the product, is $Yp(Y, A')$, Yp_2 is being paid for a marginal unit of advertising. However, the consumer saves an amount $-s_1Y$ in the form of search costs. Hence it can be stated that the level of advertising would be optimal only if $p_2 = -s_1$. This determines the A' alluded to earlier.

A further observation is in order. Suppose the level of advertising chosen by the firm is $A < A'$. Clearly, the consumer would consider it worthwhile and pay for it. That is, $p = p(Y, A)$ for $A \leq A'$ is an acceptable description of the demand curve for the firm[38]. The case where $A > A'$ wil be taken up in the sequel.

This basic departure from the received theory is necessary if welfare has to be respecified by incorporating consumer preferences for the ad-vertising level. Stated more emphatically, the Dixit and Norman (1978) approach, which takes the post advertising level of the demand curve as the standard for welfare measurement, is valid only when the A chosen by the firm is less than or equal to A'.

Note that the utility level of the consumer is generated by incurring two costs:

(a) the costs of production and selling costs incurred by the producer[39]

---

[38] It should therefore be noted that welfare comparisons based on the post advertising level of demand would be unequivocally valid if $A_\pi \leq A_w$.

[39] It may be pointed out that even firms may incur search costs in such markets in their attempts to identify the strategies of fival firms. This part of the cost can also be accounted for in the specification of $C(Y, A)$ function.

and

(b) the search costs incurred by the consumer.

Hence, the sum of these two costs is the social cost at which the utility is generated. Formally, denote

$$C'(Y, A) = \text{ total social cost } = C(Y, A) + Ys(A).$$

At relatively low values of advertising it will be expected that the cost C_2 incurred by the firm is small relative to the reduction in search cost Ys_1. Hence, there is a reduction in the social cost and a consequent increase in welfare. But, as A increases the additional information content decreases and the reduction in search cost will not be commensurate with C_2. That is, $C_2' = C_2 + Ys_1 = 0$. Let A^* be the resulting choice of A.

Note that the A^* so defined may not coincide with A'. Suppose $A^* > A'$. The cost $C'(Y, A)$ is not minimized, for a given Y, if the firm chooses $A = A'$. Consequently, welfare can be increased by moving toward $A = A^* > A'$. In fact, A^* will be the welfare maximizing level of advertising. See Fig.5.5(a). The case where $A^* = A'$ is trivial and is represented in Fig.5.5(b).

On the other hand, let $A^* < A'$. Then, given the size and organizational design of the firm, A' cannot be satisfied except at a higher social cost. In such a case $A^* \leq A \leq A'$ may be socially efficient. The case where A' is welfare maximizing is depicted in Fig.5.5(c).

Evidently, the case where $A^* > A'$ is different from the conventional analysis of the efficiency of advertising. The situation represented in Fig.5.5(c) is a hybrid of these new dimensions and the analysis of Section 5.2. Hence, the main focus of the remaining sections will be on Fig.5.5(a) alone.

One of the major reasons for the emergence of inefficiency in the

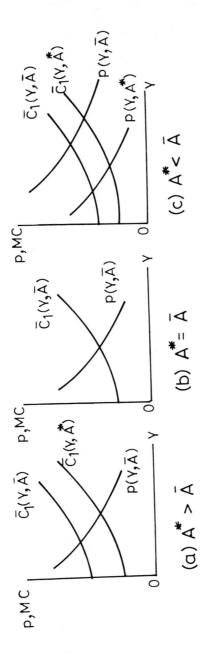

Figure 5.5. Search Costs and Advertising

choice of advertising and selling costs can be identified from Fig.5.5(a). For, in the context of monopolistic product markets, the consumers may at the most exert pressure on the firms to choose the level A' of advertising where their costs of procurement of a given Y are minimal. They may not even be aware of further welfare increases that can be achieved. The choices of the management may not correspond to the minimum social cost for various reasons.

Secondly, managerial preferences may not correspond to profit maximization in the context of such markets. Instead, they may pursue the objective of stabilizing the market share and/or maximizing sales revenue. In general, it can be shown that preference functions of the type $u = u(\pi, Y)$ necessitate the choice of A and other factors of production to minimize the costs $C(Y, A)$ for a given Y. On the other hand, the cost minimization property does not hold if the managerial preference function is of the form $u = u(\pi, A)$. This gives rise to the possibility of an inefficient choice of the level of advertising. This source has been designated as the lack of internal pressure.

The other major source of inefficiency is the lack of external pressure. For, assume that through an optimal search process the consumer defines a ceiling demand curve for each of the products in the market. However, due to their search cost limitations, some firms may operate on a higher demand curve. The consumer does not have sufficient power in the market to eliminate this possibility. This is usually the implication of the lack of external pressure. Clearly, the observed level of advertising will be inefficient even in this case. For analytical purposes, external pressure is said to exist if $p_2 = -s_2$, in addition to the assumption of free entry which is a postulate in the theory of monopolistic competition, while the lack of external pressure can be characterized by $p_2 > -s_1$.

An analysis of the inefficiency of the advertising level can therefore be developed along the lines of the earlier chapters.

5.4 EFFICIENCY OF ADVERTISING REVISITED

It is relatively easy to show that the presence of both internal and external pressure would be sufficient to ensure efficiency of advertising. For a given Y, the existence of internal pressure amounts to the maximization of a preference function of the form $u(\pi, Y)$. The resulting choice of A would be the same as that obtained by maximizing π. Since the main focus of the analysis is on the choice of A, rather than allocative inefficiency in the choice of Y, it would be simpler to assume that the firm maximizes π.

The π function will be somewhat different depending on the value of A. For, by the nature of the definition of A',

$$\pi = Yp(Y, A) - C(Y, A), \quad \text{for} \quad A \leq A', \quad \text{and}$$
$$= Yp(Y, A') - C(Y, A), \quad \text{for} \quad A > A'.$$

For a given Y, the choice of A would be such that

$$\pi_2 = p_2 Y - C_2 = 0, \quad \text{for} \quad A \leq A', \quad \text{and}$$
$$\pi_2 = -C_2, \quad \text{for} \quad A > A'.$$

Recall that for any given Y, $C_2 > 0$ for all values of A. Consequently, $\pi_2 < 0$ for $A > A'$. It follows that the actual choice of A will always be less than or equal to A'. Let $\pi > 0$ at the actual choice of A. Then, free entry of firms will begin to reduce the profit. Hence, in an equilibrium configuration A' coincides with A^* for the Y chosen by the firm. However, this is not sufficient to make the actual choice of A coincide with A^*. Existence of external pressure, defined by $p_2 = -s_1$, is necessary and sufficient to ensure such a result. For, then,

$$\pi_2 = p_2 Y - C_2 = -s_1 Y - C_2 = -C_2' = 0$$

indicating that A^* will be the chosen level of advertising. In otherwords, free entry into the market along with the operation of external and internal pressure will bring about a welfare maximizing level of advertising. The nature of the equilibrium is represented in Fig. 5.6.

It should be noted further that the choice of A implied by $\pi_2 = -C_2' = 0$ is unaffected by the changes in the elasticity of demand. The advertising decision of the firm remains efficient whatever may be the price elasticity of demand. This confirms the conjecture that the traditional notion of the inelasticity of demand as a source of inefficiency of advertising levels is inadequate.

Now consider a situation in which the firm experiences internal pressure but lacks external pressure. That is, even when free entry is postulated, incumbent firms may not find it economical to incur search costs to identify rival behavior and react to it in such a way that profits are reduced to zero[40]. Whenever this happens there may be an upward shift in the demand curve over and above the ceiling demand curve which would result from the consumer valuation of the product. The consumers themselves may not be in a position to generate the requisite countervailing power. It can be shown that the level of advertising chosen by the firm in such a situation is inefficient. Reconsider the $\pi_2 = 0$ equation. Since

---

[40] Barriers to entry, to the extent that they operate independently of search cost considerations of the firms, will add to the deviation of A^* from A' and the actual choice of A.

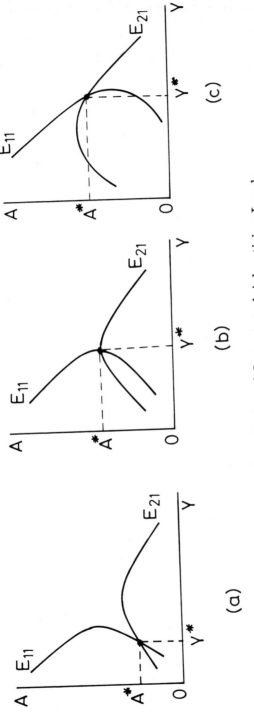

Figure 5.6. Choice of Output and Advertising Levels

114

the lack of external pressure implies $p_2 > -s_1$ it follows that

$$C_2 = p_2Y > -s_1Y, \quad \text{or} \quad C'_2 = C_2 + s_1Y > 0.$$

Consider Fig.5.7. In this figure the level of advertising that minimizes the social cost has been indicated by A^* while the profit maximizing choice is A'. Hence, it follows that the level of advertising chosen by the firm is excessive in comparison with the welfare maximizing level. Since the firm chooses A', a cost inefficiency represented by the area FGH is created. The amount of additional information that the firm provides to consumers through advertising by incurring a cost $HA^*A'F$ can be obtained by the consumers themselves by spending $HA^*A'G$ on search costs. This cost increase signals the emergence of welfare loss when the firm lacks external pressure.

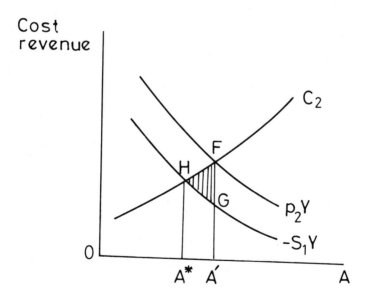

Figure 5.7. Lack of External Pressure

It would be useful to note that the advertising level being excessive can be established even if the simultaneous change in Y and A are taken into account. For, the trajectories of the first order conditions can be redrawn when $p = p(Y, A)$; $A > A^*$, $p_2 > 0$. A comparison of the values of dA/dY reveals that the trajectory becomes flatter when this slope is positive and becomes steeper elsewhere. This is represented by E_{12} in Fig.5.8. In a similar fashion it can be verified that E_{22} will be steeper when $dA/dY > 0$ and flatter otherwise. Depending on the values of π_{12} there will again be three possible positions of equilibrium. Referring to Fig.5.8 it can be noted that the equilibrium values of both Y and A increase due to lack of external pressure. The level of advertising chosen by the firm is excessive in comparison with the welfare maximizing level.

Consider the case where the firm experiences external pressure but lacks internal pressure. It can be shown that even in this case the choice of advertising level is inefficient. Assume that the firm maximizes a utility function of the form

$$U = U(\pi, A); \quad U_1 > 0, \quad U_2 > 0, \quad U_{12} > 0, \quad U_{11} < 0, \quad U_{22} < 0.$$

The utility maximizing level of A satisfies the equation

$$U_1 \pi_2 + U_2 = 0$$

which implies that

$$C_2' = C_2 + s_1 Y = \left(\frac{U_2}{U_1}\right) > 0.$$

That is, in the process of utility maximization, the firm chooses a level of advertising which differs from the welfare maximizing level. In particular, the utility maximizing choice of A will be in excess of the welfare maxi-

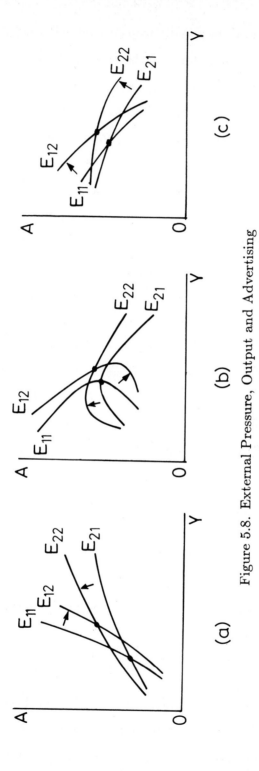

Figure 5.8. External Pressure, Output and Advertising

mizing level if $U_2 > 0$. In Fig.5.9, the area MKL represents the excessive cost involved in advertising due to lack of internal pressure[41].

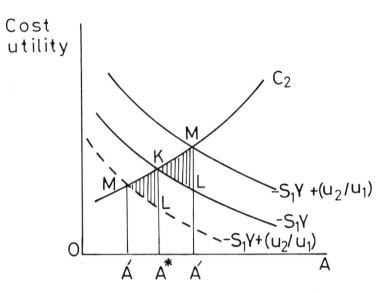

Figure 5.9. Lack of Internal Pressure

The impact of a simultaneous absence of external and internal pressure of efficiency of advertising may now be examined. With the assumptions and notation already detailed it can be shown that the choice of A satisfies the condition

$$U_1 \pi_2 + U_2 = 0, \quad \text{where}$$

$$\pi_2 = p_2 Y - C_2, \quad \text{and}$$

$$p_2 > -s_1 \quad \text{due to the lack of external pressure.}$$

---

[41] On occasions a management may consider the personal cost, to themselves, of undertaking selling strategies to be excessive in relation to their share out of the total gains for the firm. Therefore, $U_2 < 0$ cannot be ruled out at least in theory. The dotted lines in Fig.5.9 indicate that the basic result of this section wil carry over even under such an assumption. Secondly, it should be noted that so long as $U_2 > 0$ the simultaneous changes in Y and A would still be such that the level of advertising is excessive. This can be verified by a construction similar to Fig.5.8.

Hence, it folows that

$$C_2 + s_1 Y > \left(\frac{U_2}{U_1}\right) > 0.$$

It may be verified that whatever excessive advertising was there because of a reduction in either external or internal pressure, they add together if both the pressures are lacking simultaneously. Consider Fig.5.10. A^* indicates the efficient level of advertising. It is chosen by the firm when it has both external and internal pressures. The choice of the volume of advertising when there is a lack of external pressure is denoted by A'. Area FGH represents the cost increase caused by the lack of external pressure. A'' indicates the choice of A by the firm when both external and internal pressure are lacking. The inefficiency increases to the area HKL if both internal and external pressure are absent.

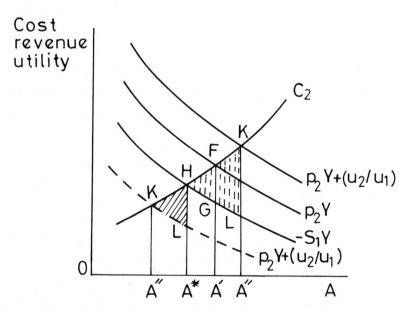

Figure 5.10 Net Inefficiency of Advertising

This completes the formal proof of the three propositions alluded to in the previous section. Thus, the level of advertising may be excessive in relation to the welfare maximizing levels due to

(a) imperfections in the product market,

(b) the incentive mechanisms and motivations of the managers, and

(c) the shelter the firm can create for itself when there is an inadequate response from the rival firms to its advertising decisions. Qualitatively, the latter two features brought out in this study are unrelated to the market imperfections. However, collectively these three aspects provide a comprehensive description of the sources of excessive advertising.

5.5 CONCLUSION

Saving consumer search cost, by providing them information about their product, has generally been acknowledged as the major motivation for the advertising activities of the firm. However, the major analytical results considered only the changes in utility functions of the consumers and neglected the search cost aspect. It has been argued in this chapter that search costs should be introduced through the budget constraint of the consumer and that this results in his expressing a specific preference for advertising. The reduction in social costs which can be expected and their welfare implications are also traced. In general, there are doubts about the minimum social cost being achieved. Market related properties, such as the inelasticity of demand and the reduction in the number of firms due to possible barriers to entry, are insufficient to explain the emergence of excessive advertising. This study has shown that two features, intrinsic to nonprice competition and the incentive mechanisms within the organization, described as internal and external pressure, are also responsible for the choice of inefficient levels of advertising.

It can generally be expected that nonprice competition becomes viable from the viewpoint of the management of the firm only if there is some increase in profits. This may also generate some increase in welfare. However, the welfare gains may not be the maximum that can be sustained in the context of such nonprice competition being undertaken by the firm. The proposition was demonstrated by an appropriate specification of both demand and cost relationships.

CHAPTER 6

TRANSACTION COSTS AND VERTICAL INTEGRATION

6.1. VERTICAL INTEGRATION AND WELFARE

Vertical integration into input production generally entails

(a) the avoidance of monopolistic price cost margins of input suppliers,

(b) a reduction in the market related and/or firm specific transaction costs, and

(c) lower costs attributable to economies of scale and scope resulting from joint production.

An appropriate analytical framework to account for all these cost reducing factors can be developed.

Carlton (1979) argued that the uncertainty inherent in bilateral bargains with input suppliers, both in terms of the prices they have to pay and reliability of supply, can be a more important motivation for vertical integration. However, uncertainty in supply and/or contractual reneging prospects can also be interpreted as an increase in transaction costs. Vertical integration provides an opportunity to reduce these costs. Thus, cost reduction remains the primary motivation for vertical integration.

Such organizational structures have significant welfare implications for the consumers of the final product of the firm[42]. Scherer (1980, pp. 300ff) argued that vertical integration increases welfare whenever there is a net reduction in cost. On the other hand, Kahn (1971, p. 255) and Williamson (1971) felt that

---

[42]Stigler (1976) pointed out that in such a case the firm can be viewed as producing two outputs and that the other inputs will be chosen to minimize the cost of both these outputs. However, the efficiency of this choice of the level of the input produced itself is not explicitly considered due to a failure to recognize that there is no explicit market for internal decisions.

(a) by exploiting the economies of scale and scope the integrated firm tends to be large, and

(b) intergrated firms may impute higher prices to the inputs which they produce while holding prices at the downstream stage constant thereby under-reporting profit opportunities.

Both these aspects create barriers to entry and result in an increase in demand for incumbent firms and a reduction in the number of firms in the market.

A vertically integrated firm may be able to convince the consumers that it is a more stable and reliable supplier. This can generate an inelasticity of demand for the products of such firms[43]. Hence, it is generally claimed that the monopoly power generated by the inelasticity of demand may be another source of reduction in welfare[44].

It will be shown that neither the lower elasticity of demand nor the reduction in the number of firms can adequately explain the expected changes in welfare. Therefore, it would be necessary to identify features intrinsic to the particular internal form of organization as the causes of the change in welfare.[45] Secondly, backward vertical integration will be perferred over the market operations only if there will be some cost reductions ex post. Perforce there is an expectation of an increase in welfare. Hence, if there is some inefficiency in the functioning of such firms it must be in terms of the actual welfare increases being less than the potential maximum which can be generated by the internal logic of such

---

[43] Note that the ability to create barriers to entry may be unrelated to the elasticity of demand.

[44] In a related context, Carlton (1979, p. 201) argued that a market structure involving vertical integration lowers the level of utility to the consumers. For, vertical integration reduces the ability of firms to pass on or share risks with the input producer and will usually result in higher prices in the input markets. It can therefore be expected that both the probability of shortage and the price of the final goods will rise.

[45] For a historic account of the survival argument and its appraisal in the context of imperfect markets see Williamson (1964, pp. 17-21).

organizational structures. It will be shown that the two new dimensions, generated by the internal logic of such organizations are related to the internal and external pressure on firms, are essential. As such this analysis is an important step in the appraisal of the welfare effects of comparative organizations within the firm.

6.2. INTERNAL AND EXTERNAL PRESSURE

The inelasticity of demand in monopolistic markets, which is a result of the uniqueness of the product, is often considered as a source of monopoly power which reduces welfare. However, referring to Fig.6.1, it can be noted that in the case of

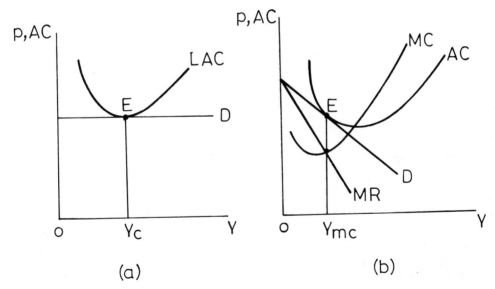

(a)   (b)

Figure 6.1. Cost Minimization and Market

(a) a competitive market, as well as

(b) monopolistic competition,

survival of the firm requires cost minimization in the long run. It can therefore be concluded that the inelasticity of demand is inadequate to account for the entire reduction in welfare.

Consider the possibility of defining the sources of inefficiency in terms of a reduction in the number of firms. Such a reduction induces a shift in the demand curve from D to D' as indicated in Fig.6.2. But there is no reason for the profit maximizing firm to deviate from the minimum AC. Consequently, it cannot be claimed that there is no motivation to reduce costs of production. Hence, the reduction in the number of firms is also not a useful description as a cause of possible welfare reduction.

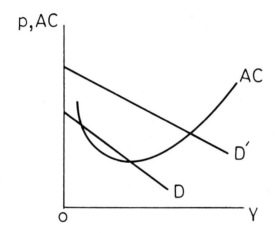

Figure 6.2. Number of Firms and Welfare

Thus, whatever may be the effect of the elasticity of demand and the number of firms on the functioning of a market they cannot have any bearing on the efficiency of the vertical integration decisions of the firm. It is necessary to consider other features of the mode of vertical integration itself to proceed with the analysis.

There is a mechanism, other than entry barriers and reduction in the number of firms, through which a firm can shift its demand curve to the right. For, the consumer may consider a vertically integrated firm to be a more reliable supplier since it does not experience input uncertainty. This can give it a market advantage.

Referring to Fig.6.3, there is a conflict between welfare maximum and profit maximum depending on the changes in the elasticity of demand. Welfare can increase if the D becomes less elastic. But lower elasticity is not conducive to profit maximization. In general, successful backward vertical integration, viewed from the perspective of profit maximization, does not maximize welfare even if it increases it.

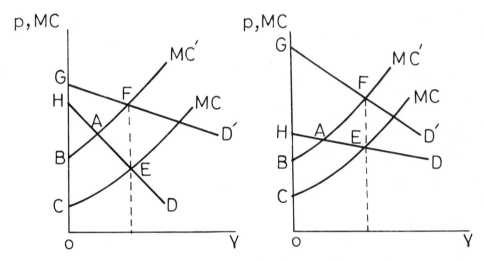

Figure 6.3. Welfare and Elasticity of Demand

Both the lack of internal and external pressures therefore increase costs above the minimum possible under vertical integration and do not maximize welfare even if some increase is discernible. An analysis of the inefficiency of vertical integration decisions can be developed by resorting to these concepts as in the earlier chapters.

6.3. Costs and Efficient Integration

Consider a single product firm in a monopolistic market. Assume that one of the variable inputs of the firm is being purchased initially from a monopolistic input market. As such it will be presumed that a sufficiently large variety of substitutable but differentiated inputs is available at different prices. Therefore, the managers will incur some costs while

(a) searching for an appropriate source of inputs, and

(b) negotiating, preparing, policing and enforcing the contract with the input supplier.

As a result, the cost of acquisition of the input from the market consists of

(a) a price paid on the market, inclusive of the marginal cost of production and price cost differential due to the monopolistic nature of the market, and

(b) the transaction costs.

Let the payments to the input supplier be represented by

$$\phi[g(Y)] = X q(X), \quad \text{where}$$
$$Y = \text{level of final output of the firm,}$$
$$X = g(Y) = \text{input required in production,}$$
$$q(X) = \text{market price for a unit of } X, \text{ and}$$
$$\phi = \text{expenditure on the purchase of input.}$$

It will be assumed that

(a) inputs are subject to diminishing marginal products so that $g_1, g_{11} > 0$ where g_1 denotes the derivative of $g(Y)$ with respect to Y, and

(b) $q_1, q_{11} > 0$ indicating increasing marginal cost of acquisition of inputs. Consequently, ϕ_1 and ϕ_{11} are positive. The market related transaction costs will be represented by

$$T = T[g(Y)], \quad \text{where} \quad T_1, T_{11} > 0.$$

That is, the transaction costs are normally expected to increase with the purchase of input quantity.

In addition to the total cost of acquiring this input the firm has to incur

(a) costs of purchasing other fixed and variable inputs, and

(b) firm specific transaction costs include the costs of information, coordinating the activities of various individuals, and monitoring the use of inputs[46].

In general, both the marginal cost attributable to the other inputs as well as the firm specific transaction costs can be expected to increase with the volume of output. The requisite specification will be reviewed presently.

Before proceeding further note that due to a variety of considerations, the managers of the firm may prefer the alternative of producing the requisite input within the firm, i.e., undertake backward vertical integration. Perforce, this arrangement would imply a change in the cost of inputs. For, on the one hand, there is an expectation of saving in transcation costs as well as monopolistic margins inherent in market exchange. On the other hand, the marginal cost, of the output firm internalizing input production, may be different from the marginal cost of the input producer.

---

[46] Upto this point the transaction cost literature has the character of positive rather than normative analysis. However, the following analysis should be sufficient to show that it can have important implications for welfare economics as well.

Assume that the firm integrates into input production. Let I be the quantum of input produced by the firm. The costs of the inputs needed for producing Y and I can then be written as

$$C' = C'(Y, I).$$

In general, C'_{12} will be negative for small values of Y and I indicating the existence of economies of joint production. As the value of Y and/or I increases, C'_{12} will become zero and it will be positive thereafter. The firm specific transaction costs can be analogously represented by

$$T' = T'(Y, I).$$

Clearly, T' exhibits properties which are similar to those of C'. However, it has been widely recognized that the nature and extent of cost complementarity arising from the organizational factors can be quite different from the technological factors. See Sharkey (1982, pp. 74ff). Hence, the distinction between C' and T' will be maintained to highlight this viewpoint.

Reconsider the costs of purchasing the input from the market after integration. Specifically, $Z = g(Y) - I$ of input has to be obtained from the market if $Z > 0$. Similarly, if $I > g(Y)$ the extra quantity $(-Z)$ will be sold on the market. The proceeds from such a sale can be considered as a reduction in the cost of production and $T(Z) = 0$ for $Z > 0$. The nature of the function $\phi(Z)$ is depicted in Fig.6.4.

The total cost function of the integrated firm can now be written as

$$C(Y, I) = C'(Y, I) + T'(Y, I) + \phi(Z) + T(Z).$$

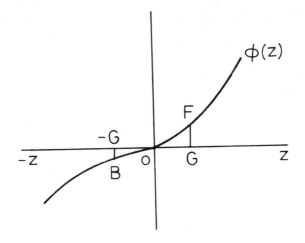

Figure 6.4. Nature of Transaction Costs

It consists of four components:

(a) costs of production within the firm,

(b) firm specific transaction costs,

(c) costs of purchasing inputs from the market, and

(d) market related transaction costs.

In general, it can be expected that $C(Y, I)$ exhibits economies of scope since both C' and T' satisfy this property. That is, $C_{12} < 0$ initially but will become positive for large values of I. Further, for a given Y, there are still some cost advantages of integration when I is small. For, the sum of the production and firm specific transaction costs $(C'_2 + T'_2) > 0$ would be less than the market related expenditure plus transaction costs $(\phi_1 + T_1) > 0$. Since $C_2 = (C'_2 + T'_2) - (\phi_1 + T_1)$ it follows that the net marginal cost associated with internalizing the production of an additional unit of input is initially negative. That is, $C_2 < 0$ for small values of I. It is this cost advantage in the initial stages of internalizing the production of an additional unit of input which provides the firm the incentive to integrate. Evidently, $C_2 > 0$ if I is rather large. That is, it can be generally postulated that $C_{22} > 0$. These are the essential properties of the cost function of a vertically integrated firm.

The specification of the maximum level of welfare that can be achieved under the mixed organizational mode may now be developed in the following manner. Firstly, note that a consumer would find the product of this firm more attractive and would be willing to pay a higher price only upto the point where it is fully vertically integrated[47]. Hence, the resulting demand curve, which represents a ceiling demand curve for the firm, can be represented by

$$p = p[Y, g(Y)].$$

The maximum welfare that can be obtained can then be shown to satisfy the equations

$$p[Y, g(Y)] = C_1(Y, I), \quad \text{and}$$

$$C_2(Y, I) = 0.$$

The choice of I is such as to minimize the cost of producing a given level of output Y. The rest of the analysis would be confined to this property of cost minimization[48].

---

[47] An alternative appears to exist. The consumer may prefer to buy from this firm if it is a minimum cost producer. The degree of integration may not be the most important consideration. Then the demand curve becomes $p[Y, I^*(Y)]$. However, the interpretation of the text is more plausible because the consumer cannot generally have much information on the production cost of the firm. Further, the rest of the analysis remains unaltered even if this alternative interpretation is adopted.

[48] During the early phases the inefficiency was defined in terms of welfare loss. But in much of the subsequent literature the emphasis is on cost minimization alone.

Hence, the efficient level of integration, for a given Y, will be defined as the value of I which minimizes the total cost of production to the firm. Such a choice of I, to be denoted by I^*, satisfies the following conditions

$$C_2 = C_2' + T_2' - \phi_1 - T_1 = 0, \quad \text{and} \tag{1}$$

$$C_{22} = C_{22}' + T_{22}' + \phi_{11} + T_{11} > 0. \tag{2}$$

It is evident that for a given Y, an increase in I entails a saving of $\phi_1 + T_1$ in market transactions while incurring an additional cost $C_2' + T_2'$ within the firm. Hence, as Coase (1937) noted, a firm should expand until the cost of organizing an extra unit of transactions within the firm is equal to the cost of carrying out the same transactions by means of an exchange on the open market.

Observe that the efficient level of I need not be equal to $g(Y)$. In fact, the economically efficient choice of I may entail a less than, equal to, or greater than the level of full integration depending on the nature of the cost function and the size of the fixed factor[49]. For, consider the first order conditions for welfare maximum. Given the assumptions made so far the trajectories of (Y, I) satisfying these equations can be represented by E_{11} and E_{21} in Fig.6.5. The intersection can occur at a point where both

(a) E_{11} and E_{21} are rising ($C_{12} < 0$),

(b) E_{11} and E_{21} have reached a maximum ($C_{12} = 0$), or

(c) E_{11} and E_{21} are decreasing ($C_{12} > 0$). It is also obvious from the definition of I^* that any deviation from it entails an increase in the total cost of producing a given volume of output Y. The question of

---

[49] This is a short run analysis. However, the result appears to carry out even in the long run so long as the input requirements function is defined independent of the cost curve. Full integration may not be efficient even if all inputs are perfectly substitutable.

whether firms would in fact choose the efficient level of integration in their actual operations can now be examined.

6.4. CONDITIONS FOR EFFICIENCY

Assume that the firm producing the final output experiences external pressure. That is, the price it can obtain for a given level of output Y is independent of the degree of vertical integration. Let the demand curve be

$$p = p(Y); \quad p_1 < 0$$

where $p =$ price per unit of Y. Postulate that the managers of the firm are subject to internal pressure as well. That is, they pursue the goal of profit maximization. Under these assumptions, the optimal choices of Y and I satisfy the equations

$$p[1 - (\frac{1}{\eta})] - C_1' - T_1' - \phi_1 g_1 - T_1 g_1 = 0 \tag{3}$$

where η is the elasticity of demand, and equation (1) of the previous section, along with the usual second order conditions. It therefore follows that, at the Y chosen by the firm, the level of integration will be efficient[50] when both external and internal pressure are present.

For the sake of further comparisons, the nature of the equilibrium has to be considered in detail. Taking the above two equations and the second order conditions into account it can be shown that the (Y, I) locus satisfying equation (3) is generally of the form represented by E_{11} in Fig.6.5(b). Similarly, equation (1) can be represented by the locus of points denoted by E_{21}. It can also be verified that E_{11} will be steeper

---

[50] The choice of Y itself is not economically efficient. But this does not, in itself, influence the cost minimizing choice of I.

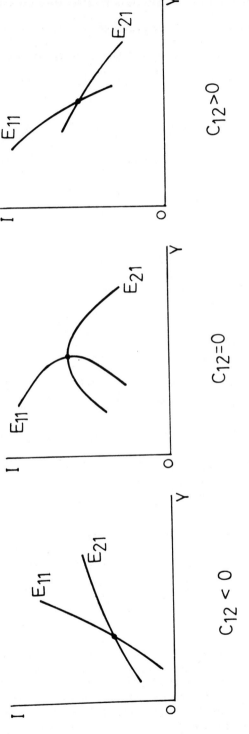

Figure 6.5. Nature of Equilibrium Y and I

than E_{21}. The equilibrium (Y, I) choice is represented by the intersection of the E_{11} and E_{21} curves. The three possible positions of equilibrium are exhibited in Fig.6.5. It is also clear that the firm will produce beyond the region of cost complementarity if the market demand for Y is sufficiently high.

As observed in the previous section, changes in the market power, if they are represented by the changes in the elasticity of demand, cannot be a source of inefficiency for a given Y. Trivially, note that equation (1), which defines the actual choice of I by the firm does not depend on the elasticity of demand. Consequently, whatever may be the elasticity of demand, the optimal choice of I for the relevant Y is always efficient[51] in the presence of both external and internal pressure.

6.5. EMERGENCE OF INEFFICIENCY

Consider the case where the internal decisions of the firm influence the market demand curve. The various reasons for the preference of buyers to purchase from an integrated firm have already been outlined in Section 6.2. When there is a lack of external pressure the demand function will have to be respecified as

$$p = p(Y, I); \quad p_1 < 0, \quad p_2 > 0.$$

Clearly, a positive value of p_2 is an indication of the reduction in external pressure[52].

---

[51] Note that there is a change in Y as η increases. However, the cost efficient choice of Y at the new value of Y alone is relevant for the present analysis.

[52] In the present context, all such preferences are created in the mind of the buyers only if the rivals are unable to compete with the integrated firm. That is, they are unable to convince the buyers that their products are equally good. The lack of external pressure is being caused by the lack of competition from the rivals.

Assume that the firm continues to experience internal pressure. The profit maximizing choices of Y and I then satisfy the equations

$$p[1 - (\frac{1}{\eta})] - C_1' - T_1' - \phi_1 g_1 - T_1 g_1 = 0, \quad \text{and}$$

$$p_2 Y - C_2' - T_2' + \phi_1 + T_1 = 0.$$

(4)

Equation (4) implies that

$$C_2 = C_2' + T_2' - \phi_1 - T_1 = p_2 Y > 0.$$

That is, due to the reduction in external pressure, the firm chooses a degree of integration which is not cost efficient. In particular, the choice of the extent of integration would be such that the internal cost of producing the marginal unit of input is higher than the cost of obtaining it on the market.

A perusal of Fig.6.6 indicates that the profit maximizing level of Y

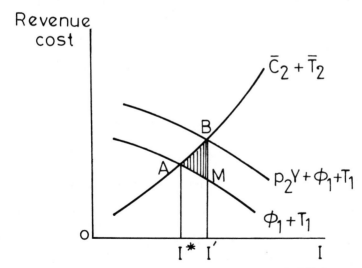

Figure 6.6. External Pressure and Efficiency

obtained under the present market conditions could have been produced with lower costs had there been external pressure. While the efficient level of integration is I^*, the firm chooses I' in the absence of external pressure. To produce I^*I' amount of additional input, the firm incurs an extra cost equal to the area $AI^*I'B$ while it would have been possible to obtain it from the market by incurring a cost equal to the area $AI^*I'M$. It is therefore obvious that the firm incurs an extra cost equal to the area AMB due to lack of external pressure.

Fig.6.7 is drawn to indicate the changes in the equilibrium values of Y and I. It is obvious that as the external pressure is reduced there will be an increase in the profit maximizing choices of both I and Y. For a given rightward shift in the demand curve a larger Y can be sustained at I^* and a larger I at Y^*.

It was noted earlier that in the case of large firms operating in monopolisitc market environments the motivation to maximize profits may be reduced either due to the attenuation of property rights or due to the design of incentive mechanisms for internal organization. In either case the utility function of the managers can be represented by

$$u = u(\pi, I) = u^*(Y, I)$$

where $u =$ level of utility. As in the earlier chapters this will be considered as the specification of the lack of internal pressure.

Assume that the firm faces external pressure so that the impact of the lack of internal pressure can be isolated. The first order conditions for utility maximization can now be written as

$$p[1 - (\frac{1}{\eta})] - C'_1 - T'_1 - \phi_1 g_1 - T_1 g_1 = 0$$
$$C_2 = C'_2 + T'_2 - \phi_1 - T_1 = \frac{u_2}{u_1}. \tag{5}$$

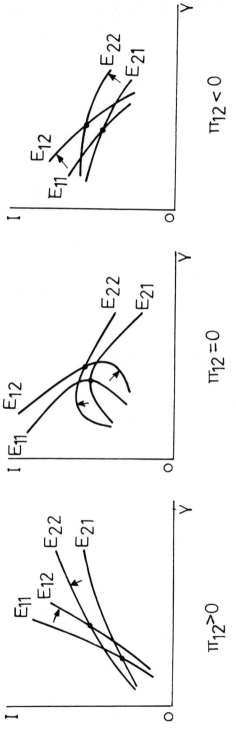

Figure 6.7. External Pressure and Equilibrium

That is, the firm which lacks internal pressure will also integrate to an inefficient level of I for the Y it chooses. The ratio (u_2/u_1) can be considered as the degree of lack of internal pressure. Further, recall that $C_{22} > 0$ at the efficient level of I^*. See equation (2). Consequently, any deviation from I^* corresponds to an excessive cost of production. Hence, the choice of I is inefficient whatever may be the sign of u_2.

Fig.6.8 is drawn to indicate the extent of cost increase due to the lack of internal pressure in the simple case where the ratio (u_2/u_1) is

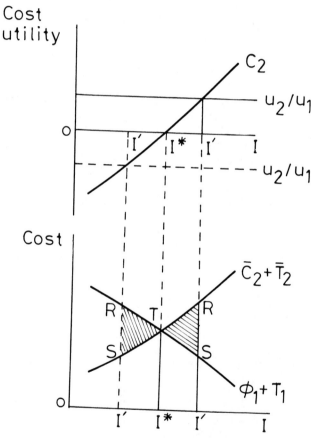

Figure 6.8. Internal Pressure and Efficiency

constant for all values of I. It may be noted that the degree of inefficiency of integration increases with the extent of reduction in internal pressure. In particular, the area TRS represents the increase in the total cost of producing Y due to the lack of internal pressure. It is fairly obvious that the inefficiency due to internal pressure would be greater than that caused by external pressure if $(u_2/u_1) > p_2 Y$.

It can now be shown that a simultaneous reduction in both the pressures has an additive effect on inefficiency. For, in this case, the first order conditions can be reduced to

$$p[1 - (\frac{1}{\eta})] - C_1' - T_1' - \phi_1 g_1 - T_1 g_1 = 0, \quad \text{and}$$
$$C_2 = C_2' - T_2' - \phi_1 - T_1 = p_2 Y + (\frac{u_2}{u_1}). \tag{6}$$

Equation (6), in comparison to (4) and (5), establishes the validity of the proposition. Clearly, even when $u_2 < 0$, the effect of the lack of internal pressure would be purely coincidental. Persistence of inefficiency is the more likely outcome.

Referring to Fig.6.9, note that the firm integrates upto I^* when both the pressures are present. Lack of external pressure moves it upto I' and the movement is to I'' if both external and internal pressures are lacking. The amount of excessive cost incurred due to the lack of both external and internal pressures is represented by the area LFH.

This completes a formal proof that the absence of internal and/or external pressure leads to economic inefficiency in the vertical integration decision.

6.6. CONCLUSION

Saving market related transaction costs has been generally acknowledged as the major motivation for vertical integration into input markets.

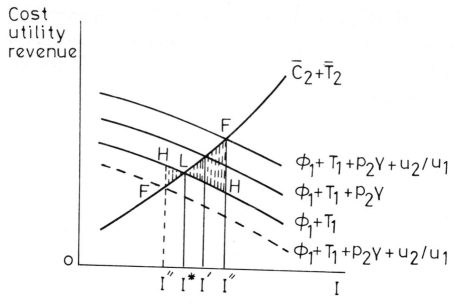

Figure 6.9. Net Inefficiency in the Choice of I

However, there have been doubts about this organizational design sustaining the minimum possible cost. Market related properties, such as the elasticity of demand and the reduction in the number of firms due to possible barriers to entry, are insufficient to explain the emergence of inefficiency in internal organizational modes. This study has shown that two features, intrinsic to the organization and incentive mechanisms contained within it, described as internal and external pressure, are responsible for inefficiency. Analysis of the welfare effects of organizational structures can be systematized on this basis.

The notion of inefficiency which can be sustained in such organizational contexts only indicates that the potential maximum welfare gains may not be achieved. There is however an increase in welfare beyond the purely market mode. As such it cannot be a condemnation of the mixed organizational forms. At best it can suggest that the design of internal organization and/or incentive mechanisms within it can be improved. Any suggestion that returning to the purely market mode would be superior appears to be unwarranted.

CHAPTER 7

INVENTORY DECISIONS

7.1. THE BASIS FOR INVENTORY HOLDING

Almost throughout the theory of monopolistic competition it has been acknowledged that the market conditions would be such that

(a) the size and scope of the firm will have to be sufficiently large to enable it to adopt an effective policy of product differentiation, and

(b) there is an under utilization of production capacity.

The firms in this market would therefore find that there can be significant reduction in dynamic costs of production if they utilize capacity more fully and/or diversify into related products[53]. Such cost reduction strategies will necessitate utilizing inventories.

In general, the demand curves for the products of the firms in this market are affected by

(a) the environmental conditions external to the firm and industry, and

(b) actions and reactions of rival firms within the industry.

Such changes in the demand curves may be

(a) systematic and anticipated, or

(b) unanticipated and fluctuating.

Even these variations in market demand indicate that static choices of production levels, in response to an observed demand at every point of time, would not be optimal from the viewpoint of maximizing profits over more than one period of time.

---

[53] One of the strategies of such firms is to make an attempt to stabilize the demand curve through advertising and other features of product differentiation. These have already been considered in Chapter 5.

Figure 7.1 serves to illustrate the point. Consider, for purposes of analytical simplicity, decision making over two periods of time. To begin with assume that D_1 and D_2 are the demand curves in the market during the two periods of time and that they are known with certainty[54]. Postulate that the costs of production are unaltered between the two periods of time. If the firm makes independent production decisions in the two periods of time under consideration it will choose quantities Y_1 and Y_2 respectively. For purposes of analysis assume that Y_2 is significantly higher than Y_1. Then, the firm incurs a high average cost of production $Y_2 A_2$ in period 2. However, note that the firm has the option of producing a larger quantity, say Y_a, in period 1 and reducing production by an equivalent amount to Y_b in period 2. That is, $Y_1 Y_a = Y_b Y_2$. It is at once evident that the firm may incur

(a) an extra cost of production in period 1 on even the Y_1 units of output, and

(b) the cost of carrying a quantity $Y_1 Y_a$ forward in their warehouses.

Against this cost the firm has the advantage of reducing the cost of producing each of the Y_b units of output in period 2. Evidently, such a production policy has the prospect of yielding a larger combined profit relative to the decision of keeping the two periods of production isolated. The quantity $Y_1 Y_a = Y_b Y_2$ will be labelled F and will be designated as the final good inventory. A similar analysis applies even when the firm experiences change in costs from one period to the next.

Randomness in the demand curves can likewise impose large fluctuations in the production level and consequent costs of adjustment. Even under these conditions the firms would generally find it worthwhile to

---

[54] This analytical procedure is valid even in the context of firms operating in a competitive product market. It is important to note this in order to appreciate the validity of the welfare comparisons under different market structures.

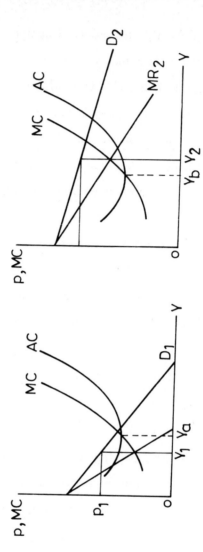

Figure 7.1. Justification for Inventories

reduce costs by smoothing out production and adopting an appropriate inventory policy.

Underlying the motives for adopting an inventory policy is another aspect of these fluctuations in demand. In general, products of different firms in the market are close substitutes of one another. Hence, if a particular firm experiences a stock out and cannot satisfy market demand then there is a loss of goodwill which will affect its future profit possibilities as well. As a result of this there can be a tendency to hold inventories as a precautionary measure.

Laregeness of size and optimal inventory holding by incumbent firms may also have the effect of increasing the cost of entry. In particular, a firm which has a large enough inventory can temporarily reduce price to drive out an entrant. Even from the consumer viewpoint a firm with an adequate inventory may be a more reliable supplier[55]. In other words, a firm may be able to maintain a steady demand or increase it by using a suitable inventory policy.

Despite the pervasive occurence of inventory decisions economic theory has remarkably little to indicate the fundamental connection between microeconomic theory and inventory decisions. There are many reasons for this.

(a) The static theory of the firm uses marginal analysis as its corner stone. Such an approach is usually straightforward and most useful if there are no time dependent demands or costs. But this condition is not satisfied in inventory analysis. For, as noted earlier, the value of inventory holding to a firm is precisely that it can be utilized for

---

[55] This argument may go the other way around also. Consumers may view the firm
  (a) as a high cost firm,
  (b) as supplying an unreliable product, or
  (c) as one who charges a higher price. Any one of these features can create a disadvantage for the firm.

generating profits in the future.

(b) When time dependence in the decision making process is acknowledged the problem can be analyzed only by taking the entire decision problem over the plan horizon as a single unit. Marginal concepts are not available to appreciate the nature of the solutions.

(c) Most of the inventory systems actually found in operation assume a given price structure and assume a strictly cost minimizing approach. The simplicity of the use of these methods has itself become its disadvantage. For, no attempt has been made to see if these short cut decision rules can be justified on any microeconomic foundations. In the early stages Whitin (1955) made an unsuccessful attempt. It has not been followed up since and it does not appear to be promising even now.

With this background in perspective the present chapter will systematically develop a theory of decision making with respect to production and inventory within the framework of the microeconomic theory of a monopolistic firm. A simple diagramatic approach and marginal analysis will be utilized at the cost of some generality.

7.2. IMPACT OF INVENTORIES ON WELFARE

To the extent that inventory holding stabilizes production levels over time it will be expected that a cost reduction can be achieved. This is the most important source of increases in welfare. Nguyen (1976), Hey (1979), Arvan and Moses (1982), Phlips (1983), Loury (1983), Breshnahan (1985), Arvan (1982), and others noted this result. However, in imperfect product markets the firms may not have the incentive to reduce the costs to the minimum so long as there is no threat to survival. Hence, as with other organizational decisions of the firm, an increase in welfare, though it is likely to occur, will not be the maximum possible.

When firms fix production levels ex ante and smooth production over time there are possibilities of

(a) the demand not being met, or

(b) wasteful excess if inventory holding is not possible or it is extremely expensive.

However, when inventory holding is possible and the firms derive profit from such a policy it would be possible to satisfy even fluctuating demands. This, in itself, contributes to an increase in welfare. The consumers of the product may have an implicit valuation for inventory over and above the demand for the product itself. To an extent it may be expected that in some markets this consumer valuation exceeds the inventory costs and contributes to increases in welfare. However, as before, there is a possibility that the level of inventory, structured to smooth costs of production over time, may not be commensurate with the consumer preferences.

Wright (1984) suggested that the management of the firm expresses a demand for inventory by paying an explicit storage cost for it. To this extent, they can be said to increase welfare over and above the improvements in the profit position. However, it is not altogether clear if any such concept of welfare is tenable. For, the utility to the management, of holding inventories, consisits of only the possibility of increasing its profits dynamically. Further, if the neoclassical concept of welfare, alluded to in Chapter 2, is maintained this definition of welfare is unacceptable.

It was also pointed out by Wright (1984) and others that the possibility of inventory holding may result in a favorable valuation of the firm's products by the consumer. This is a result of the reduction in the opportunity costs of wastage. The consumer can be said to have an implicit demand for inventory[56]. However, it is apriori difficult to decide whether this results in "higher elasticities of demand" as Wright (1984) claims or to lower elasticity of demand and increased monopoly power for the firm. If the latter possibility is taken into account there can be a reduction in welfare.

On certain occasions, confronted with demand fluctuations, monopolistic firms may hold inventories for purely speculative purposes. Cost minimization is not necessarily attempted under such conditions and the possibility of welfare loss cannot be underestimated.

Phlips (1983) argued that entry of new firms into the market can be expected whenever the incumbent firm is deriving profits from inventory holding. However, the established firms in the market may fix lower prices for their products and/or overstate the accounting or logistic costs of inventory thus understating the profit potential and creating a barrier to entry. If this were to happen there would be a loss in welfare.

Inadequate reactions of rivals and the lack of external pressure can occur even dynamically. This will be a source of welfare reduction as in the previous chapters.

On balance, it may be claimed that despite the possibility of some increases in welfare actually materializing, the inventory policies of firms do exhibit aspects of inefficiency emphasized in the foregoing chapters. A systematic examination of these details is therefore warranted.

---

[56]On occasions, it was pointed out that the consumers have to hold an inventory on their own if the producers do not. The motivation is to avoid shortage of supply when there are uncertainties. Invariably this would be more expensive. Hence, it would be rational for them to pay a higher price for the security of supply brought about by the firm holding inventories.

7.3. MARGINAL CONCEPTS

An attempt will be made in the present section to examine the production and inventory decisions within a marginal framework by concentrating on the final goods inventory. The simplification of a two time period horizon is mostly for analytical simplicity. It can be shown that analogous concepts can be generated even in a more general dynamic model.

Without any loss of generality, the conceptual base can be developed by utilizing the following pertinent assumptions:

	Period 1	Period 2
Production	Y_1	Y_2
Cost of Production	$C(Y_1)$	$C(Y_2)$
Demand Curve	$f(S_1)$	$g(S_2)$
Sales	$S_1 = Y_1 - F$	$S_2 = Y_2 + F$
Inventory	F	0
Inventory Cost	$h(F, Y_1)$	0

Three observations are in order:

(a) it is convenient to assume that inventory is not carried beyond the first period. This assumption may be relaxed by postulating that the firm wishes to attain a predefined target level at the end of the second period. The optimality, or otherwise, of such a choice, if explicitly introduced into the analysis, would complicate presentation without any new concepts emerging,

(b) a multi-period model can be thought of as being condensed into a two-period analysis by considering the present discounted value of transactions beyond the first period. But, this interpretation, though plausible apriori, involves many conceptual problems, and

(c) dynamic cost considerations, even if important, will not be explicitly taken up. The simpler version is more instructive. For, the economic mechanisms underlying the decision structures can be exhibited forcefully.

An appropriate specification of the inventory cost function is crucial to the analysis. It can be developed in the following manner. Let Y_1 units of output be produced during time period 1. However, F units of this output, held back in the form of inventory, are not sold during this time period. The cost of production incurred $= FA(Y_1)$, where $A(Y_1) =$ average cost of producing a unit of Y_1. Assume that this money is borrowed from the banks or some other source. Interest must be paid on this amount irrespective of whether the expenses are recovered or not. Given F, the level of inventory, an increase in Y_1 can be expected to result in an increase in $A(Y_1)$ and consequently the interest cost of inventory holding increases. Similarly, it should be noted that given a Y_1 an increase in F results in an increase in the interest costs. In addition, there is a storage cost. This increases with F. Consequently, the inventory holding cost $h(F, Y_1)$ is such that $h_1 > 0$, and $h_2 > 0$.[57] Observe that in a situation where $F = 0$ the costs of carrying inventories as well as the associated costs will be zero. This result holds irrespective of the level of production.

---

[57] It is possible to observe $h_2 < 0$ if $A(Y_1)$ decreases with Y_1 due to the existence of unused excess capacity and economies of scale in production.

Hence, h also satisfies the conditions

$$h(0, Y_1) = 0, \quad h_1(0, Y_1) = 0, \quad \text{and} \quad h_2(0, Y_1) = 0.$$

Keeping these aspects in perspective, consider an increase in Y_1 holding F and Y_2 constant. This results in the following changes in revenues and costs for the firm[58]:

(a) there is an increase in the cost of production given by $C_1(Y_1)$,

(b) there is an increase in inventory cost equal to $h_2(F, Y_1)$, and

(c) there is an increase in revenue which can be represented by

$$f(Y_1 - F)[1 - (\frac{1}{\eta_1})],$$

where η_1 is the elasticity of demand in time period 1.
Hence, the Y_1 choice maximizes profit only if

$$f(Y_1 - F)[1 - (\frac{1}{\eta_1})] = C_1(Y_1) + h_2(F, Y_1). \tag{1}$$

Further, at the margin, the marginal costs must be increasing more than the marginal revenues to satisfy the second order conditions for profit maximization with respect to Y_1. Hence, generally it can be expected that the gains from the inventory policy outweigh the costs so that

$$F f_1(Y_1)[1 - (\frac{1}{\eta_1})] + h_2(F, Y_1) < 0. \tag{2}$$

Expanding the left hand side of equation (1) in Taylor's series and rear-

---

[58] No explicit discounting procedure is being adopted. However, it can be verified that all the results of this and the following sections carry through even if discounting is introduced.

ranging terms it follows that Y_1 is optimal only if[59]

$$MR = f(Y_1)[1 - (\frac{1}{\eta_1})]$$

$$= C_1(Y_1) + F f_1(Y_1)[1 - (\frac{1}{\eta_1})] + h_2(F, Y_1)$$

$$= MCP.$$

MCP is a representation of the marginal cost of increasing production in the presence of an appropriate inventory policy.

Given the assumptions of equation (2) it can be concluded that in general $MCP < MC$ whenever there is a positive inventory holding.

It should be noted, for purposes of consistency, that if

$$F = 0, \quad h_2(F, Y_1) = 0$$

since there is no cost of inventory. Under these conditions MCP reduces to MC and the static monopoly situation is restored.

Similarly, if $MCP > MC$, output is reduced below the static level and sales of period 1 are conducted from the beginning of period inventory, if any.

The marginal cost of sales can now be defined in an analogous fashion. Consider an increase in F by one unit given Y_1 and Y_2. Such a decision results in

(a) a decrease in S_1 and a decrease in revenue by

$$f(Y_1 - F)[1 - (\frac{1}{\eta_1})],$$

(b) an increase in inventory cost equal to $h_1(F, Y_1)$, and

---

[59] Note that Y_1 is plotted on the horizontal axis when drawing the diagram for the optimal choice of Y_1. Hence, MR is expressed as a function of Y_1. Similarly, the marginal cost of production will be expressed as a function of Y_1 and F.

(c) an increase in S_2 and an increase in revenue by

$$g(Y_2 + f)[1 - (\frac{1}{\eta_2})].$$

Hence, the choice of F will maximize profits only if

$$g(Y_2 + F)[1 - (\frac{1}{\eta_2})] = f(Y_1 - F)[1 - (\frac{1}{\eta_1})] + h_1(F, Y_1). \qquad (3)$$

Rearranging terms, it follows that[60]

$$MR = f(Y_1 - F)[1 - (\frac{1}{\eta_1})]$$
$$= g(Y_2 + F)[1 - (\frac{1}{\eta_2})] - h_1(F, Y_1)$$
$$= MCS \qquad (4)$$

where MCS is the marginal cost of sales.

Note that $MR_1 = MR_2 = MC$ and $MCP = MC = MCS$ if there is an identical demand position in both time periods and there is no advantage in holding any inventory.

It would now be pertinent to examine the position of MCS relative to MCP. Consider the difference

$$MCP - MCS = C_1(Y_1) + Ff_1(Y_1)[1 - (\frac{1}{\eta_1})] + h_2(F, Y_1)$$
$$- g(Y_2 + F)[1 - (\frac{1}{\eta_2})] + h_1(F, Y_1).$$

Suppose the second period demand is higher than the first. Then, it is very likely that $Y_2 > Y_1$. Hence, the marginal revenue in the second period

---

[60] In this case S_1 is plotted on the horizontal axis. Hence MR is expressed as a function of S_1. Similarly, MCS is a function of S_1 and F.

should be more than adequate to cover the marginal cost. That is,

$$C_1(Y_1) - g(Y_2 + F)[1 - (\frac{1}{\eta_2})] < 0.$$

Further, the cost of inventory holding for an additional unit of inventory can be expected to be less than the interest on the production cost itself. That is,

$$h_1(F, Y_1) - h_2(F, Y_1) < 0.$$

Consequently, it is possible to have

$$MCP < MCS.$$

This inequality will be reversed if the first period market is better.

The optimal choices of Y_1 and F are represented in Fig.7.2. In particular, Fig.7.2(c) represents the possibility of increasing sales by drawing down the initial inventory stock whenever it is available.

The optimal choice of Y_2 can now be shown to satisfy the equation

$$g(Y_2 + F)[1 - (\frac{1}{\eta_2})] = \text{marginal revenue in period 2}$$

$$= \text{marginal cost in period 2}$$

$$= C_1(Y_2). \tag{5}$$

Thus the marginal concepts provide a convenient analytical procedure for examining the inventory decisions of firms.

7.4. WELFARE MAXIMIZATION

It is possible to define welfare costs of production and sales by adopting a procedure analogous to that of the previous section. For, let Y_1 and

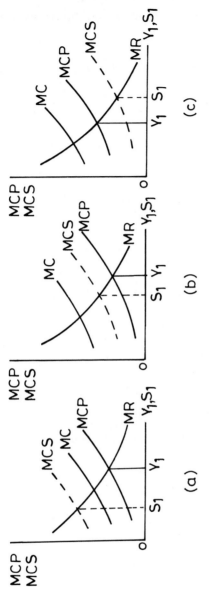

Figure 7.2. The Marginal Concepts

Y_2 be fixed. Consider an increase in S_1 by 1 unit. This has the following effects:

(a) contribution to welfare in time period $1 = f(Y_1 - F)$

(b) reduction in inventory cost $= h_1(F, Y_1)$

(c) reduction in welfare in time period $2 = g(Y_2 + F)$.

Hence, the choice of S_1 is welfare efficient only if

$$f(Y_1 - F) = \text{price per unit of sales } S_1$$
$$= g(Y_2 + F) - h_1(F, Y_1)$$
$$= \text{welfare cost of } S_1$$
$$= WCS. \tag{6}$$

However, the efficiency of the choice of S_2 requires that

$$g(Y_2 + F) = C_1(Y_2).$$

This is the familiar price $=$ marginal cost rule for welfare maximization. From (6) it follows that

$$WCS = C_1(Y_2) - h_1(F, Y_1). \tag{6'}$$

Similarly, substitution of equation (5) into (4) results in

$$MCS = C_1(Y_2) - h_1(F, Y_1). \tag{4'}$$

Two observations are pertinent:

(a) given Y_1, Y_2 equations (4') and (6') are identical. That is, whatever may be the elasticities of demand the choice of F for a given Y_1, Y_2 will be welfare efficient.

(b) If $\eta_1 = \eta_2 = \infty$ the profit maximizing choices of Y_1, Y_2 coincide with the corresponding welfare maximizing choices. The actual choice of F would not then contain even the allocative inefficiency induced by the choice of output levels.

Somewhat more generally consider the welfare and profit maximization requirements explicitly. Maximizing the two period welfare function

$$W(Y_1, Y_2, F) = \int_0^{Y_1} f(Y_1 - F)dY_1 + \int_0^{Y_2} g(Y_2 + F)dY_2 - C(Y_1)$$
$$- C(Y_2) - h(F, Y_1)$$

yields the first order conditions

$$f(Y_1 - F) - C_1(Y_1) - h_2(F, Y_1) = 0$$
$$f(Y_1 - F) - g(Y_2 + F) + h_1(F, Y_1) = 0, \quad \text{and}$$
$$g(Y_2 + F) - C_1(Y_2) = 0.$$

It follows from these equations that the welfare maximizing choice of F, given Y_1, Y_2, satisfies the equation

$$f(Y_1 - F) = g(Y_2 + F) - h_1(F, Y_1). \tag{7}$$

However, from equation (4) the profit maximizing choice of F would be such that

$$f(Y_1 - F)[1 - (\frac{1}{\eta_1})] = g(Y_2 + F)[1 - (\frac{1}{\eta_2})] - h_1(F, Y_1).$$

Hence, if the product market is competitive, these two conditions are identical and the choice of F would be economically efficient.

In monopolistic market situations the choice of output levels exhibits an allocative inefficiency. Consequently the choice of F would be inefficient. However, it is apparent that for given Y_1, Y_2, the profit maximizing choice of F is economically efficient. For, invoking the welfare maximizing condition for Y_2, viz.,

$$g(Y_2 + F) = C_1(Y_1)$$

equation (7) reduces to

$$f(Y_1 - F) = C_1(Y_2) - h_1(F, Y_1).$$

Hence, it follows that

$$C_1(Y_1) + h_2(F, Y_1) = C_1(Y_2) - h_1(F, Y_1) \tag{8}$$

will be satisfied by the efficient choices of Y_1, Y_2, and F. However, the profit maximizing choices of Y_1, Y_2, and F implied by the equations (1), (3) and (5) are also such as to satisfy equation (8). The only difference is that Y_1, Y_2 are not the same. Further, this condition does not depend on the values of the elasticity of demand. Hence, it can be concluded that, given Y_1, Y_2, the choice of F is economically efficient for all values of η_1 and η_2.

The inefficiency in the choice of F in monopolistic markets is due to the inefficient choice of Y_1, and Y_2. The allocative inefficiency carries over to the inventory decisions as well. There can be no other source of inefficiency when both external and internal pressures are postulated.

7.5. Other Sources of Inefficiency

It can now be briefly demonstrated that the absence of external and/or internal pressure adds to the inefficient choice of the level of inventory which the firm holds.

Let the management of the firm lack internal pressure. Instead, postulate that they are willing to tradeoff some profit to reduce their loss of goodwill by adopting an inventory policy. That is, their preference function can be written as

$$u = u(\pi, F); \quad u_1 > 0, \quad u_2 > 0.$$

The choice of F and the implied level of sales S_1 is now governed by the equation

$$u\left(\frac{\partial \pi}{\partial F}\right) + u_2 = 0.$$

Consequently,

$$-\frac{\partial \pi}{\partial F} = -\frac{u_2}{u_1}.$$

hence, the change in the marginal cost of sales can be expressed by

$$f(Y_1 - F)\left[1 - \left(\frac{1}{\eta_1}\right)\right] = g(Y_2 + f)\left[1 - \left(\frac{1}{\eta_2}\right)\right] - h(F, Y_1) + \left(\frac{u_2}{u_1}\right)$$
$$= MCS + \left(\frac{u_2}{u_1}\right)$$
$$= MCS_u \quad \text{(say)}.$$

Obviously, $MCS_u > MCS$ for any given S_1. This is represented in Fig.7.3.

Clearly, there is an increase in cost over the economically efficient level. As before, this leads to an inefficiency implicit in the market structure itself.

Assume, next, that the firm has been able to create a market shelter for itself through its inventory policy. This lack of external pressure manifests itself in the form of a change in the demand curve. Let the demand curve in time period 2 change to

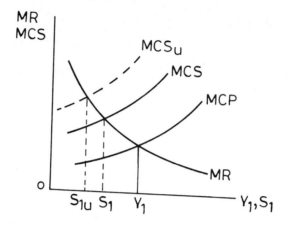

Figure 7.3. Managerial Choices and Inventory

$$p_2 = g[(Y_2 + F), F]; \quad g_1 < 0. \quad g_2 > 0.$$

Assuming that the management maximizes profits it follows that the choice of S_1 would be such as to satisfy the equation

$$f(Y_1 - f)[1 - (\frac{1}{\eta_1})] = g[(Y_2 + F), F][1 - (\frac{1}{\eta_2})] - h_1(F, Y_1)$$
$$+ (Y_2 + F)g_2[(Y_2 + F), F]$$
$$= MCS^* \quad (\text{say}).$$

Once again it is evident that $MCS^* > MCS$. From Fig.7.4 it may be inferred that the lack of external pressure also has the effect of

(a) increasing the cost,

(b) creating an inefficiency in the choice of F, and

(c) generating an inefficiency in Y_1 over and above the allocative inefficiency.

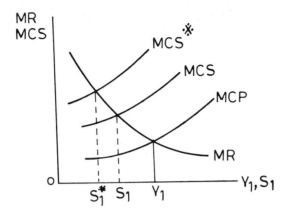

Figure 7.4. External Pressure and the Choice of S

This completes a formal presentation of the basic propositions regarding the sources of inefficiency. The intertemporal dependence in decisions is not itself a fundamental contributing factor.

It should however be obvious that the introduction of the inventory policy may reduce costs below the static levels experienced by the firm when the decisions of different time periods are kept isolated. Inefficiency in the operation of the inventory policy only indicates that the maximum possible cost savings and welfare gains are not being achieved.

7.6. MULTIPERIOD GENERALIZATION

In Section 7.1 it was noted that inventory policies of firms are dynamically related over many time periods so that a two period model can only be looked upon as an analytical simplification. However, it can be shown that the concepts of MCP and MCS, which are central to the analysis of the previous sections, carry over to the multiperiod context as well.

Postulate that

$$p(t) = f(S, t)$$

where $p(t)$ = price per unit of sales, and S = quantity of sales. Assume that the cost of production can be written as

$$C = C(Y)$$

where Y = output produced at time t. Let F be the level of inventory at any point of time t. Then, the changes in inventory from one period to the next can be represented by

$$\frac{dF}{dt} = Y - S.$$

The inventory costs will again be written as $h(F, Y)$ and the properties of this function are the same as before.

The profit for the firm at any point of time t will then be

$$\pi(t) = Sf(S, t) - C(Y) - h(F, Y).$$

Let r be the rate of discount. Then, the firm can be viewed as choosing Y and S so as to maximize the present discounted value of profits. That is,

$$\pi^* = \int_0^\infty e^{-rt}[Sf(S, t) - C(Y) - h(F, Y)]dt$$

subject to

$$\frac{dF}{dt} = Y - S$$

and suitable boundary conditions[61].

The solution to the problem can be obtained by constructing the Hamiltonian

$$H = e^{-rt}[Sf(S,t) - C(Y) - h(F,Y)] + \lambda(Y - S)$$

where λ is a Lagrange multiplier. λ can be interpreted as the discounted present value of the profit generating potential[62] of an additional unit of inventory held at time t. Then, by an application of Pontryagin's (1962) maximum principle the optimal choices satisfy the equations

$$\frac{d\lambda}{dt} = -\frac{\partial H}{\partial F} = e^{-rt}h_1(F,Y) \tag{9}$$

$$\frac{\partial H}{\partial Y} = -e^{-rt}[C_1(Y) - h_2(F,Y)] + \lambda = 0 \tag{10}$$

$$\frac{\partial H}{\partial S} = e^{-rt}f(S,t)[1 - (\frac{1}{\eta})] - \lambda = 0. \tag{11}$$

Eliminating λ from (10) and (11) by utilizing (9) it can be verified

---

[61] It is well known that there are certain non-negativity and other constraints on the decision process. See, for instance, Arvan and Moses (1982), Arvan (1985), and Boadway (1985). The basic result of this section is however adequate for the present purposes.

[62] Blinder (1982) interprets this λ as an opportunity cost of holding inventories. However, the present approach appears to have the advantage of a more direct economic interpretation of the choices of the firm. Further, as already pointed out earlier, the marginal concepts are analytically far more elegant compared to Blinder's approach using the value of λ.

that the choice of Y will be such as to satisfy

$$f(Y,t)[1 - (\frac{1}{\eta})] = MR$$

$$= C_1(Y) + h_2(F,Y) + [1 - ((\frac{1}{\eta})]f_1(Y,t)(\frac{dF}{dt})$$

$$+ (\frac{1}{r})f_2(S,t)[1 - (\frac{1}{\eta})]$$

$$= MCP$$

and in an analogous manner the optimal sales at any point of time will be chosen such that

$$f(S,t)[1 - (\frac{1}{\eta})] = MR$$

$$= C_1(Y) + h_2(F,Y) + (\frac{1}{r})f_2(S,t)[1 - (\frac{1}{\eta})]$$

$$= MCS.$$

The choice of F would be according to the equation

$$r[C_1(Y) + h_2(F,Y)] = -h_1(F,Y). \tag{12}$$

The following results may now be noted:

(a) $MCP = MCS = MC$ whenever $dF/dt = 0$. That is, during that interval of time the volume produced and sold will coincide,

(b) $dF/dt > 0$ and inventory accumulation will occur whenever $MCS > MCP$, and

(c) If $f_2 = 0$ and as such the demand curve is the same over each of the time periods, inventory accumulation will not be justifiable and $F = 0$. $MCP = MC = MCS$ is also then satisfied.

In sum, the generalized concepts of MCP and MCS will exhibit the same properties as in the two period case.

In the context of welfare maximization the notions of WCP and WCS can be developed in an analogous manner. No new results emerge. It is pertinent to remark that the F choice would once again satisfy equation (12). Since this equation does not contain any η it follows that given Y the choice of F would be welfare maximum irrespective of the nature of the product markets itself. The only inefficiency in the choice of F, in the presence of both internal and external pressure, would be through the allocative inefficiency in the choice of Y.

All other results can be developed by making the necessary changes.

7.7. IN RETROSPECT

Despite the dynamic nature of the inventory decisions the two basic motivating forces, as in the vertical integration case, are

(a) the possibility of cost reduction, and

(b) avoidance of the risks posed by market uncertainties.

If the management is motivated by profit maximization in their choices of production and inventory then cost minimization will be maintained so long as there is external pressure. There is only an allocative inefficiency in the choice of Y generated by market imperfection.

However, when extra profits can be generated, the management may be induced to divert a part of it to create a market shelter to attenuate the impact of uncertainty. The management may consider this to be a preferable response in comparison to price competition itself. Whenever this happens the minimum possible costs are no longer attained. That is, the choice of inventory policy would be a compromise between the stabilization requirements and cost reduction. The maximum possible welfare is no longer attainable even if there is an increase beyond the case where the firm makes static production decisions. The inefficiency

CHAPTER 8

HIERARCHICAL ORGANIZATIONS

8.1. A CHANGE IN EMPHASIS

Upto this point in the analysis the emphasis has been on the non-price decisions of the firm. Technological efficiency of production has been taken for granted throughout the analysis. This can be stated in more concrete terms. Let x_1, x_2 be any two inputs in the production of Y and let

$$Y = f(x_1, x_2)$$

be the neoclassical production function. Then the choices of inputs is technologically efficient if the management chooses x_1, x_2 along the isoquant for a given Y. It was assumed throughout the analysis that the management is motivated to choose the input combinations along the isoquant.

Given the market prices of x_1 and x_2 there exists a minimum cost at which each of the output quantities can be produced. One of the requirements of economic efficiency is that the firms operate at the minimum cost configuration. However, it was pointed out that the separation of ownership from control and the consequent lack of internal pressure on management may have the effect of the management choosing input combinations which do not minimize the cost of production. There was however no indication that the input choices may not be along an isoquant. Instead, technical efficiency was assumed to prevail.

In a similar manner, given a cost curve, an economically efficient level of output was defined. Lack of internal pressure and/or external pressure was considered as a source of an inefficient choice of the level of output and the corresponding configuration of nonprice decisions. Once again it was postulated throughout the analysis that the management has complete information about the production function and that they operate along the neoclassical isoquants.

It is often claimed that in complex organizations the management may not have

(a) an adequate knowledge of the production functions,

(b) an incentive to operate along an isoquant, and/or

(c) a mechanism of monitoring and incentives to enforce the productivity implicit in the neoclassical production function.

In other words, technical inefficiency can also be a problem in complex hierarchical organizations. This aspect of the problem needs a closer examination.

Assume, to begin with, that the neoclassical production function is well-defined. The workers may however be unionized and cause labor problems and disrupt production[63]. In such a case, in addition to the cost disadvantages of the firm the management may experience a disutility of resolving conflicts. As a result they may feel that for a given Y of output, reducing x_2 will increase their net welfare. For illustrative purposes let the production function be

$$Y = (x_1 x_2)^{1/2}.$$

Then, given Y and x_2 the minimum x_1 needed is Y^2/x_2. An increase in x_1 beyond this may be desired to reduce labor problems. However, as x_2

---

[63] Leibenstein (1966, 1980) and elsewhere argued that the workers do not always give their best and that this causes the production to be off the isoquant. The consensus, as of now, is that this will not be organizational or managerial inefficiency. Only when certain managerial decisions induce such behavior can such notions arise. The question of making these distinctions in an empirical context are formidable.

is reduced a further increase in x_1 contributes less and less to the increase in managerial utility. Hence, it may be postulated that the managerial preference functions are of the form

$$u(x_1) = a_1(x_1 - \frac{Y^2}{x_2}) + a_2(x_1 - \frac{Y^2}{x_2})^2.$$

Clearly, $a_1 > 0, a_2 < 0$. Maximizing u with respect to x_1 results in

$$a_1 + 2(a_2 x_1 - \frac{Y^2}{x_2}) = 0$$

implying that the choice of x_1 would be

$$x_1 = (\frac{Y^2}{x_2}) - (\frac{a_1}{2a_2}) > (\frac{Y^2}{x_2}).$$

There would be a tendency on the part of the management to operate off the isoquant and accept a certain amount of technical inefficiency.

It might be argued that the management cannot ignore the consequences of their choices of x_1 on the cost of production even if they are able to tradeoff some cost of production to increase their personal gains. That is, the preference function may take the form

$$u^*[(p_1 x_1 + p_2 x_2), u(x_1)]; \quad u_1^* < 0, \ u_2^* > 0.$$

Then the choice of x_1 would be such that

$$p_1 u_1^* + u_2^*[a_1 + 2a_2(x_1 - \frac{Y^2}{x_2})] = 0, \quad \text{or}$$

$$x_1 = (\frac{Y^2}{x_2}) - (\frac{a_1}{2a_2}) - (\frac{p_1 u_1^*}{2a_2 u_2^*}).$$

It can no longer be stated unambiguously that the choice of x_1 will be off the isoquant though the possibility does exist.

Essentially this indicates that certain economic factors which enter into the decision making process may yet create technical inefficiency. The immediate observable effect is on the cost structure of the firm and the concommitant output changes and their welfare effects. From an analytical viewpoint the dilemma would be whether this should be labelled as technical or economic inefficiency. The problem of quantitatively delimiting the two is also quite formidable.

In almost all practical situations the assumptions

(a) that the production function is fully known, and

(b) that the lower level managers and the workers can be made to give their maximum productivity are unrealistic. For, as the organization grows in size the necessity to obtain and process information increases. Similarly, the need for structuring appropriate incentive mechanisms and the necessity for monitoring are greater.

Under such conditions, the management may experience

(a) a limit on their capacity to collect and process information, and

(b) information impactedness in the sense of not having the requisite information.

Consequently, the management considers the increasing costs of

(a) information assimilation, monitoring and incentive schemes, in contrast to

(b) the loss of productivity and the resulting technical inefficiency.

In a majority of cases the management may choose the latter course of action due to the advantages in

(a) their own disutility calculations of more rigorous control, and

(b) economic cost advantages.

Thus, even in situations where the neoclassical cost functions can be defined for complex organizational structures it would be unrealistic to expect these to be the standards for welfare comparisons. Instead, cost functions will have to be redefined taking into account the motivations of the various productive teams in the firm, the costs of information and monitoring and the optimal incentive mechanisms. From an analytical viewpoint this leaves a great deal of judgement and conceptualization of alternative organizational schemes.

Primarily it would therefore be possible to demonstrate the emergence of managerial inefficiency due to the lack of internal pressure given the structure of the organization, monitoring and incentive mechanisms. Examining the efficiency of alternative organizational forms on a similar analytical foundation is somewhat ill-defined and hazardous. This chapter and the next one will highlight the analytical process but cannot be considered as the final word on these problems.

8.2. SIZE AND ORGANIZATION

Modern industrial units have two distinct features:

(a) complexity of technology, and

(b) largeness of size in terms of output as well as workforce.

Complexity of technology generally requires a functional specialization of different physical operations in the production process. The owner then delegates the supervision and management of specialized activities to specific individuals. The owner (general manager) concentrates only on monitoring the other managers. Even the largeness of size suggests that one manager cannot be expected to coordinate decision making for all the diverse lines of production and the large workforce. Most firms consider decentralized hierarchical form of organization and decision making to be imperative.

Such an organizational structure has the virtue of improving the efficiency of decision making and performance of the firm. However, there are certain forces operating within such hierarchies which can lead to inefficiencies. Firstly, as the information necessary for decision making is transmitted through various levels of the hierarchy there will be distortions and inability to monitor and promptly correct noncompliance. That is, there will be a loss of control. Secondly, the managers at each and every hierarchical level cannot assess their contribution to the overall profit of the enterprise due to the lack of appropriate information. Perforce they would be pursuing more narrowly defined objectives in their decision making process. As a result there would be a cumulative inability on the part of the owner to elicit an optimal performance from the workers at the different levels of hierarchy.

Such an analysis indicates the possibility that there may be certain features of the organizational structures which account for the lack of adequate control and the resulting inefficiencies. These problems will have to be viewed as distinct from the allocational inefficiency imposed on the firm by external, and in most cases, uncontrollable market conditions.

An attempt can now be made to develop a simple model of hierarchical organization and examine the effect of loss of control due to informational difficulties on the efficiency of decision making.

8.3. THE BASIC MODEL

Following Williamson (1967, 1970) consider a firm in which there are n hierarchical levels. Let the production workers be at the lowest or the n-th level and the general manager be at level 1. The higher level workers will be assumed to handle only managerial and administrative functions. Let the span of control[64] at each level of hierarchy be s. That

---

[64] Variations in s at different levels of hierarchy have been examined by Beckmann (1983), Calvo and Wellisz (1984) and Hess (1983).

is, there are s workers of an immediately lower level working with each person in the organization[65]. It follows that

$$N_i = \text{number of workers at the } i\text{th level of hierarchy}$$
$$= s^{i-1}; \quad i = 1, 2, \ldots, n.$$

Let the degree of compliance at the ith hierarchical level indicate the degree to which the general manager's goals are executed. It is expected that compliance decreases with a movement towards the lower levels of hierarchy. Let α^{i-1}; $0 < \alpha < 1$ represent the degree of compliance at the ith hierarchical level. Then the total output Y of the firm can be expressed as

$$Y = (\alpha s)^{n-1}.$$

Consider the variable cost of production next. It may be divided into a wage component and a non-wage component. The wage rate per worker at the ith level of hierarchy will be postulated to be

$$w_i = w_0 \beta^{n-i}$$

so that w_0 is the wage rate of the production workers. It follows that the total wage bill is

$$\sum w_0 \beta^{n-i} s^{i-1}$$

which can be approximated by $w_0 s^n / (s - \beta)$ if $s > \beta$. Similarly, it will be assumed that the non-wage costs are r per unit of output. Hence, the

---

[65]Subsequent work of Keren and Levhari (1979) generalized these results. However, the Williamson formulation will be utilized throughout this chapter.

total variable cost becomes

$$TVC = \frac{w_0 s^n}{(s - \beta)} + r(\alpha s)^{n-1},$$

The average variable cost of production is therefore

$$AVC = r + [\frac{w_0 s}{(s - \beta)}]\alpha^{1-n}$$

which decreases with an increase in n. This is the basic efficiency proposition of hierarchical organizations[66].

For illustrative purposes assume that the demand curve of the firm is of the constant elasticity form so that

$$p = (\alpha s)^{-\eta(n-1)}$$

where $(1/\eta)$ is the elasticity of demand.

Two choices are available to the general manager:

(a) the size of the firm denoted by n, and

(b) the degree of compliance which can be elicited.

It is worthwhile to examine the technical as well as economic efficiency induced by market conditions in contrast to the managerial inefficiency in their decision making process.

However, in contrast to the results of the earlier chapters, the choices of n and α of the firm have only an effect on the cost conditions of the firm and cannot be expected to give the firm any sort of market advantage. In other words, considering the lack of external pressure as a source of inefficiency does not appear to be warranted. Therefore, the lack of internal pressure will be the main focus of attention.

---

[66] A choice of n to minimize the average cost of production cannot be defined due to the monotonicity of AVC. However, a welfare maximizing n can be defined in the usual neoclassical framework.

8.4. CHOICE OF THE FIRM SIZE

For purposes of this section it will be postulated that s and α are held constant by managerial choices. Consider the welfare maximizing choice of n. The welfare function can be explicitly written as

$$W(n) = \int_0^Y p(y)dy - C(Y)$$

where $Y = (\alpha s)^{n-1}$,

$$p(Y) = Y^{-\eta}, \quad \text{and}$$
$$C(Y) = \frac{w_0 s^n}{(s - \beta)} + rY$$

so that the welfare maximizing n satisfies the equation

$$(Y^{-\eta} - r)(\frac{dY}{dn}) = \frac{w_0 s^n \ln s}{(s - \beta)} \tag{1}$$

where $\ln x$ is the natural logarithm of[67] x.

In an analogous fashion the profit maximizing choice of n can be obtained by maximizing

$$\pi(n) = Y^{1-\eta} - C(Y).$$

That is, such an n satisfies the condition

$$[Y^{-\eta}(1 - \eta) - r](\frac{dY}{dn}) = \frac{w_0 s^n \ln s}{(s - \beta)}. \tag{2}$$

For any given value of the elasticity of demand η the choices of Y implied by equations (1) and (2) are different. The corresponding choices of n are also distinct. This signals allocative inefficiency.

---

[67] When this approximate form of the demand function is adopted the welfare maximizing n is independent of Y as the market becomes competitive.

However, it should be noted that n is fixed if Y is given. Hence, the existence of internal pressure suggests that the choice of n itself would be efficient for a given Y. The inefficiency in the choice of n is induced by the market imperfections alone.

Assume that the management derives satisfaction from larger size as postulated in Penrose (1959) and Williamson (1964,1970). Let

$$u = u(\pi, n); \quad u_1, u_2 > 0$$

denote the managerial preference function. Corresponding to this the optimal choice of n would be such that

$$u_1(\frac{d\pi}{dY})(\frac{dY}{dn}) + u_2 = 0.$$

Consequently the inefficiency in the choice of Y contains both an allocative inefficiency induced by the market as well as managerial inefficiency induced by $u_2 > 0$.

From this analysis it can be inferred that the lack of internal pressure adds to the allocative inefficiency in the choice of n. However, this result is somewhat different from that of the earlier chapters. Or, in the context of the other nonprice decisions considered so far the lack of internal pressure induced a cost increase which in turn manifested itself in the form of a change in Y. In contrast, the present analysis suggest that the average cost increase and the inefficiency in the choice of Y are simultaneous and concommitant. This is usually designated as the inert area hypothesis.

8.5. COMPLIANCE AND MANAGEMENT

An attempt will have to be made to define the welfare maximum choice of α for a given n and s.

Consider the welfare function

$$W(Y) = \int_0^Y Y^{-\eta} dY - C(Y)$$

where Y and $C(Y)$ have been defined earlier. Then, the α which maximizes W satisfies the equation

$$Y^{-\eta} - r = 0, \quad \text{or}$$
$$\alpha = \frac{r^{-1/\{\eta(n-1)\}}}{s}. \tag{3}$$

If the management experiences internal pressue they will choose α to maximize

$$\pi = Y^{1-\eta} - C(Y)$$

which yields

$$(1 - \eta)Y^{-\eta} - r = 0. \tag{4}$$

Consequently there is an allocative inefficiency in the choice of Y. The inefficiency in the choice of α depends only on the market conditions.

Consider the possibility that the management finds the effort necessary to increase α to be disproportionate to the returns expected for themselves. Then the management may modify their preferences and maximize

$$u = u(\pi, \alpha); \quad u_1 > 0, \ u_2 < 0.$$

As a result of this the choice of α is altered according to the equation

$$[(1 - \eta)Y^{-\eta} - r](\frac{dY}{d\alpha}) = -(\frac{u_2}{u_1}). \tag{5}$$

A comparison of equations (4) and (5) readily indicates that there is a further change in α and a corresponding inefficiency in the choice of α resulting from managerial preferences.

Thus the basic result of the previous section is valid even in this case.

8.6. Conclusion

In general it can be expected that the managers at every heierarchical level view their job as one of obtaining the maximum degree of compliance from the workers at one level below them subject to their own effort wage relationship. In practice, the labor markets at the higher levels of hierarchy are well organized and may cause a change in wages disproportionate to their productivity. The observed increases in the average costs are then a result of the operation of the external market process and cannot be designated as mangerial inefficiency. On the other hand, there is a possibility that beyond a certain level of effort individual decision makers do not consider the results of their efforts to be commensurate with the disutility of effort. Inaction resulting from this behavioral pattern may leave the average cost at a level higher than the minimum that can be attained.

Essentially this analysis serves to illustrate the view that there can be differences between the workers and the management in the choice of α. There is no organizational mechanism to equilibrate the system described in this chapter. In such cases the management may not be capable of eliciting the desired compliance. This can also become a source of inefficiency.

However, so long as the market prices can be made to correspond closely to the lowest average cost of production the management of the hierarchical organization can be expected to reduce the inert areas of operation and maintain maximum internal efficiency.

CHAPTER 9

INFORMATION, MONITORING AND INCENTIVES

9.1. THE ISSUES

Unified governance (organization) within a firm can be explained in terms of the following features:

(a) A group of individuals come together to perform certain tasks[68],

(b) As the organization becomes large and complex there is a necessity to clearly define division of labor and implement coordination of work through delegation of authority within the organization[69],

(c) Decision making is faciliated by information exchange and monitoring the performance, and

(d) Incentive payment schemes are devised from the perspective of certain well defined organizational goals.

Three aspects of such organizations make the problem of allocating resources and coordination of activities within the firm difficult.

(a) There are no market prices to direct activities within a firm. The requisite activities may have to be performed and coordinated by the visible hand of the management at various levels.

(b) Managers and workers at different levels in the heirarchy may have specialized information or expertise concerning particular spheres of activity. Usually this information is not available to other individuals within the firm including top management.

---

[68] Extensive discussions of a variety of reasons for this can be found in Coase (1937), Williamson (1979), FitzRoy and Muller (1984), Alchian and Demsetz (1972), Ackerman (1986), Berle and Means (1968) and others.
[69] These arguments are well known. For a succint statement the reader may refer to Chandler (1962,1967), Burton and Obel (1984, Ch. 4), and Radner (1986).

(c) Individuals with private information also have interests which may diverge from those of the firm and may find it disadvantageous to reveal their privileged private information to the management[70].

In essence, as Harris et al. (1982) emphasized, both

(a) the asymmetry of information at various levels of management[71], and

(b) the differences in the motivations and the objectives of the workers at different levels of hierarchy, may have to be accepted as a reality in the decision making process.

From a practical viewpoint, what the management can do is to choose an allocation of resources, which is optimal from their vantage point, keeping in perspective the information they have about the lower levels of hierarchy. However, such an allocation may not be optimal in the presence of asymmetric information since it fails to exploit the more complete information available at the lower levels of hierarchy. It may not be consistent with the expectations of the lower levels either. The alternative available to them is to delegate decision making with respect to production organization and certain other decisions to the lower levels of hierarchy. The lower levels may, in turn, utilize favorable information advantages to exploit the higher level of management. But they experience an information asymmetry with respect to markets and profit position.

---

[70] Knight (1951, p. 22) provided one of the early statements on these issues. The differences in the objectives and the general nature of the moral hazard was initially emphasized in the financial context by Berle and Means (1968) and was popularized by the literature on the principal-agent problem which was systematically formulated by Jensen and Meckling (1976).

[71] Langlois (1984) considered three types of information problems:

    (a) the full extent of alternatives available for a given transaction are unknown,

    (b) it is not possible to anticipate the strategies that will be used in bargaining and the terms which are offered, and ,

    (c) it is difficult to accurately identify the deviations from the contract. It is well known that the bounded rationality arguments consider the other dimensions of this problem.

This can result in inefficient decisions. Hence, in either case, the concept of an efficient resource allocation as well as the process through which it can be achieved are in doubt.

It is therefore essential to define the organizational structure, the information and monitoring systems, the incentive mechanisms and the decision rules (contractual processes) in order to ascertain the degree to which the divergent interests of the different groups in the organization can be satisfied. Stated somewhat differently, signalling by subunits, information flows across subunits, monitoring of activities, as well as the incentives offered to different subunits can be said to affect the economic behavior within organizations.

The present chapter considers the simplest organization where the activities of a single group of workers is coordinated and directed by a manager. It is argued that a simple budget negotiation process does not necessarily lead to an efficient equilibrium position. This result holds even when information uncertainty is posited so long as the assumptions, of information asymmetry and differences in the motivations of the two groups, are maintained. A case can, therefore, be made for monitoring and incentive schemes to obtain an increase in efficiency. It is then demonstrated that despite some possible improvements in the cooperative solutions, the prisoner's dilemma problem persists. On the whole, it is shown that both the parties, in the contract and exchange, accumulate information regarding

(a) motivations and the degree of cooperation that can be elicited from the other group, and

(b) the uniformity and impartiality in dealing with the group behavior.

The various organizational units develop the necessary cooperative responses on such a basis. Managerial inefficiency is endemic to such organizations.

9.2. BASIC RESPONSE TO INFORMATION ASYMMETRY

Consider a simple two-level organization in which one manager (M) is coordinating the activity of a single group of workers (G)[72]. Following Hoenack (1983, p. 21) it will be postulated that

(a) the group has been delegated the authority for the application of all the productive inputs required to manufacture a single final product. The group has complete knowledge of its production function, ie., the input output relationships. Let the production function[73] be written as

$$Y = f(B, e), \quad \text{where}$$

$$Y = \text{output produced,}$$

$$B = \text{budget used by } G \text{ to produce } Y, \text{ and}$$

$$e = \text{level of personal effort of the group } G.$$

However, the manager does not have any accurate knowledge of this production domain.

(b) The manager has complete information regarding the market for the

---

[72] More general formulations of hierarchical organizations, in a similar context, failed to highlight the issues which will be considered in this chapter. See, for instance, Calvo and Wellisz (1978), Hess (1983) and Mirrlees (1976). However, it would appear that the present formulation would carry over to even these generalized organizational contexts.

[73] The conventional way of writing this is $Y = f(x_1, x_2)$, where $x_1 = $ fixed factor, and $x_2 = $ variable factor (say labor). If effort (e) is a variable itself, the actual labor input to production is ex_2 and $Y = f(x_1, ex_2)$. The budget B for the purchase of x_1 and x_2 is $B = q_1 x_1 + q_2 x_2$, where q_1 and q_2 are the input prices. Hence, it would be convenient, for the present purposes, to write $Y = f(B, e)$. Slightly more general formulations are adopted in the section entitled Monitoring the Group.

output produced by the group. However, as implied in the postulate of information asymmetry, the group does not have adequate market information.

The objectives of the two levels of hierarchy will also be postulated to be different. In particular,

(a) the management is primarily interested in the profit that accrues to them. They will be postulated to maximize a preference function

$$u = u(\pi); \ u_1 > 0, \quad \text{where}$$

$$\pi = \text{ profit for } M, \quad \text{and}$$

$$u_1 = \frac{du}{d\pi}$$

π can, in turn, be written as

$$\pi = p(Y)Y - B, \quad \text{where}$$

$$p(Y) = \text{ price per unit of output.}$$

(b) The group of workers can determine the level of effort needed to produce a given Y since they know the production domain. This will be a function of Y and B, viz.,

$$e = e(Y, B); \quad e_1 > 0, \quad e_2 < 0.$$

For a given amount of effort, an increase in B implies greater gains to the group. Similarly, it can be expected that any reduction in e would be apriori desirable from the viewpoint of G. Consequently, it may be postulated that the welfare of the group is

$$v = v(B, e); \quad v_1 > 0, \quad v_2 < 0.$$

It may therefore be observed that for both M and G there is a relationship between B and Y in their decision making process. In particular,

(a) the group demands $B = B(Y, v)$ as the budget required to produce output Y when they want to attain a level of welfare v, and

(b) the management is willing to offer $B = B(Y, u)$ for the same level of Y if they wish to achieve a level of welfare u for themselves.

Notice that from this definition of the u function it follows that

$$\frac{dB}{dY} = p(Y)[1 - (\frac{1}{\eta})]$$

where η is the elasticity of demand for Y. Hence, the slope of the u-curves in the (B, Y) plane depend on the nature of the market. In particular, they will be flat if the elasticity of demand is high. On the other hand, the slope of the v-curves in the (B, Y) plane are such that

$$\frac{dB}{dY} = -\frac{v_2 e_1}{(v_1 + v_2 e_2)}$$

so that this is primarily determined by the motivations of G and is unrelated to the product market characteristics. Note that both these slopes are positive under the assumptions made so far. It is necessary to examine their relative magnitudes. The v-curves will be steeper than the u-curves if the worker's group is very ambitious and does not recognize the low profitability of a competitive product market. The obverse holds if the worker group is submissive. It should also be noted that the group G derives greater welfare for a given Y if B increases. On the other hand, the management obtains a larger u whenever B can be reduced for a given Y.

9.3. Welfare Maximization

One of the basic difficulties in examining the efficiency of organizational decisions is the definition of the welfare maximum itself. In the present context the consumers can be viewed as maximizing their level of satisfaction keeping the compliance of workers in perspective[74]. Consider the welfare function

$$W(Y) = \int_0^Y p(y)dy - B$$

where the output Y is produced by the group at a contracted cost B. Unlike the neoclassical situation, in which $B = C(Y)$ is a well defined cost function, the choice of B is determined by organizational choices. There is no ex ante specification of B as a function of Y even if it is ex post. The choices of Y and B which maximize welfare cannot be specified unless the budgetary negotiation between the consumers and the worker group G is explicitly taken into account. For, this would implicitly take the budgeting process between the workers and the management M into account. Thus, the economic efficiency of the choice of a specific organizational form is itself an important consideration.

Let W be fixed at a specific value. Then, considering B as a function of Y it follows that

$$p(Y) - \left(\frac{dB}{dY}\right) = 0$$

---

[74] This notion is consistent with neoclassical economics where the owner manager is considered as a residual claimant. The alternative would be to define optimal (Y, B) contracts between the consumers and managers (in market exchange) on the one hand and the management and the workers on the other. Notice that the price which the consumers would be made to pay would depend on the B and it is for this reason that they will consider B in the negotiation. It there is a single cooperative solution which is acceptable in both exchanges welfare maximum is easy to define. In general this should not be taken for granted. The difficulty would then be to define welfare maximum.

or $B = B(Y)$ is positively sloped in the (B, Y) plane. Secondly, given a Y, an increase in B reduces welfare. Hence, the welfare level increases as the isowelfare contours move to the right. Thirdly, if the worker's group does not fully recognize the limitations of the product market while defining its budgetary demands then the v-curves will be steeper than the w-curves. This is represented in Fig.9.1.

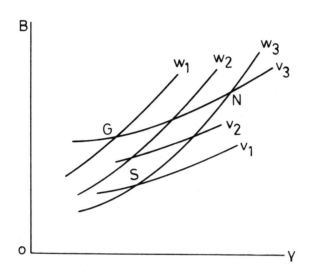

Fig.9.1. Preferences of Management and the Group

Assume that v_1 is the reservation level of utility for the worker group. That is, they would prefer to seek employment elsewhere if the value of v is sought to be reduced below this. Then the society would prefer to choose the (B, Y) combination represented by S to maximize welfare[75]. Similarly, given an expenditure B the society would at least like to generate a level of utility equal to B. In comparison to other alternative productive activities on which to spend the budgeted amount

[75]It is being assumed that $B(Y)$ increases faster than w_1/w_2 as Y increases. Under this assumption there exists a maximum w_3 that can be attained.

188

there can be a positive reservation level w_1. If it is now assumed that the group has the better bargaining power the equilibrium would be at the point G. However, notice that a cooperative solution, such as N, would be Pareto superior. Hence, even though it entails a higher average cost of production compared to B, the society may be better off accepting[76] that choice of N. The welfare maximum should be defined accordingly.[77]

The management has the option of monitoring the use of the resources by the group and/or provide incentive mechanisms to move toward the optimum budgets from their own viewpoint[78]. However, it will be presently shown that this modification does not alter the fundamental nature of the problem of managerial inefficiency.

9.4. BUDGETS AND CONTRACTING

Budget negotiations between the management and the workers can be expressed in terms of the u and v functions since the output Y can be observed by both G and M. However, the equilibrium is not determinate as yet. For, many values of B and Y appear to be candidates for negotiated settlement. Consider Fig.9.2(b). In this figure the demand for the budget is drawn for several levels of welfare of the group and the willingness of M to offer B is drawn for different welfare levels of u. Given

---

[76] Leibenstein's (1966, 1980) argument, that the effort of the workers not being the maximum is a source of inefficiency, is discounted if this position is adhered to. This is generally the position of Alessi (1983) and others.

[77] A Nash equilibrium, if it exists, may be considered as an alternative specification of the welfare maximum. The qualitative nature of the results of the following sections would not change materially.

[78] It should be noted that issues pertaining to the distribution of gains between

   (a) the workers,
   (b) the management,
   (c) the owners and shareholders, and
   (d) the consumers is always an important issue in defining the welfare maximum. The position being taken here is that a negotiated and cooperative solution, if it can be arrived at, would be the feasible choice. This is a contestable premise.

the budget B_1 the manager notices that the group is more than willing to offer the Y expected and that its own level of welfare is low. The management may try to renegotiate so as to increase u attained under the threat of replacing the group if they do not compromise. Hence, it is possible that u and v will adjust in such a way that a more acceptable equilibrium materializes. In the short run, however, the worker group is not satisfied when budget B_2 is being offered. Hence, the management may have to compromise and offer a larger budget even if it reduces their welfare to some extent. This suggests that the ultimate equilibrium will depend upon the relative bargaining powers of G and M. A similar argument holds even in the context of Fig.9.2(a).

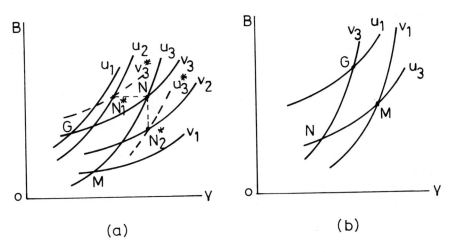

(a)   (b)

Figure 9.2. Negotiation and Welfare

Assume that G is strongly unionized and can enforce its will on M. Then, they will reduce the gains to M to the lowest reservation level, u_1 say. Referring to Fig.9.2 the point G represents the ultimate choice of B and Y as a result of bargaining. Similarly, M would be the equilibrium if the management is relatively more powerful and v_1 represents the reservation level of welfare for group G below which they would prefer to seek employment elsewhere.

Fig.9.2 however indicates the possibility that negotiated solutions may make at least one of the parties in the contract better off. Let N be the point of intersection between u_3 and v_3. Since a movement toward N, starting from either G or M, is a better solution for at least one of the parties either one of them may initiate an approach to such a cooperative solution. Fig.9.2(b) is a situation in which any movement away from N represents a strong conflict between the parties so that both of them may prefer the status quo at a lower level of equilibrium. Stagnation and decay are preferred by both G and M in some organizations since they are unable to compromise with each other on their paths of growth and progress.

However, the cooperative solution N in Fig.9.2(a) may not materialize. For, suppose a cooperative solution such as N is agreed upon. But the manager may eventually offer only a lower payment say at N_2^*. Then the group loses since they cannot attain v_3 any longer. However, the management gains by moving to $u_3^* > u_3$. Similarly, the group may produce a smaller Y at N_1^* and reduce the welfare of the management to u_2 while increasing its own welfare to $v_3^* > v_3$. The cooperative solution is subject to this kind of reneging and moral hazard and it is not stable. This prisoner's dilemma may reduce welfare since the more powerful group, G or M as the case may be, imposes its maximum on the other party. N itself may never be achieved due to a lack of trust in the other party adhering to the contractual solution. Such organizations are highly conflict prone.

Further, there is no scope for any monitoring in the (B, Y) model because the management provides B and observes that Y is actually produced. Neither can the management observe the effort level of G nor can they get to know how B is actually spent. Similarly, the group does not know what profit the M is able to generate by selling the output[79].

9.5. MONITORING THE GROUP

In the foregoing analysis it has been assumed that the workers adjust their effort level, for a given level of output Y, and negotiate the budget with the management accordingly. In other words, the worker's demand for a budget is determined by the subjective valuation of the group. This is the general approach of the organizational behavior literature adopted by the psychologists. Leibenstein (1980, 1987) extended this tradition to economic analysis. However, Hoenack (1983) argues that the objective factors, underlying a given demand for budgets, are far more fundamental. The effect of monitoring and incentives, on organizational behavior, can also be examined in such a framework.

The fundamental postulate of such an approach is the distinction between the actual production domain of the workers (about which they have complete knowledge) and their perceptions about the management's knowledge regarding the production function. It is assumed that the management has incomplete (and perhaps uncertain) information about it when they delegate production responsibility to the group. This is one important dimension of information asymmetry under which management operates. It gives rise to an opportunity for the group to exploit the

---

[79] Information asymmetry has been modelled in some studies through game theoretic rationality. The principal agent problem is the typical structure of such formulations. For a diagramatic exposition of this aspect, one can refer to Hirschleifer and Riley (1979). The emphasis in this approach is to accept the presence of uncertainty and design efficient decision rules. These will usually be designated as incentive compatible mechanisms. The alternative is to make attempts to obtain information and resolve uncertainty as far as possible before defining decision rules. This framework is adopted here. The conclusions remain broadly the same irrespective of the approach adopted.

management for its own advantage. In particular, refer to Fig.9.3. In this figure, z_1 and z_2 are two inputs in the production process and it is assumed that both of them are purchased on the market[80]. The production domain Y_g of the group indicates that an output Y can be produced at a cost C_g. But, due to information asymmetry, the group anticipates that the management would consider production to be possible at M at a cost C_m. It is this cost differential, $M^* = C_m - C_g$, which the group can convert to its own advantage[81].

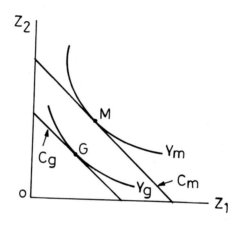

Figure 9.3. Information Asymmetry

However, in the presence of monitoring, especially budgetary allo-cations and audits, the entire M^* cannot be converted into cash for use of the group. Whatever amount they cannot convert in this manner may then be utilized to generate on the job leisure. In other words, the group will try to convert M^* into the form of cash resource diversions (D) or cost

---

[80] If one of them is labor then the effort problem reappears. Similarly, if one or more of the inputs is internally produced there will be information asymmetry in the transfer price mechanisms. The basic analysis of this section can be extended to such cases as well. For simplicity of exposition it will be assumed that both parties have an accurate information regarding the market prices of these inputs.

[81] Note that this proposition is symmetric with the argument of Coase (1937) regarding managerial behavior in the presence of transaction costs in the use of markets.

increases above $C_g(\Delta C)$ which arise due to the on-the-job leisure component. In general, of course, the behavior of the group is constrained by
$M^* = \Delta C + D$.

Notice that the greater the ΔC the better off the group will be
because they can experience greater on-the-job leisure. Similarly, the
group attaches a positive marginal value to increases in D as well. The
preference function of the group, $v = v(\Delta C, D)$ will then be convex in the
$(\Delta C, D)$ plane as usual. Referring to Fig.9.4 the point E of tangency is
the preferred position of the group. This may involve positive values of
both ΔC and D.

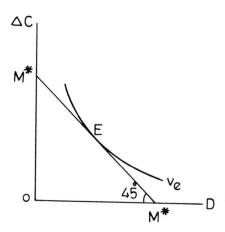

Figure 9.4. Resource Diversions

Notice that the point O in this figure corresponds to G of Fig.9.3.
The pertinent question is: Can the group be monitored so that they
choose O as their optimal decision? Since the management is aware that
its knowledge of the production domain is imperfect it will try to offer
a low enough budget to reduce resource diversions and cost increases.
However, the outcome of such budgetary negotiations will be primarily

determined by the nature of the preference function v of the worker's group.

The primary effect of monitoring of this nature is one of placing a lower limit on the amount of resources which the group can divert and thereby altering the maximum level of v that they can attain. This will not, in general, be effective enough to reduce their choices to the point M of Fig.9.2. Similarly, the additional information available to the management may enable them to raise the minimum level of welfare they can attain. The starred values of Fig.9.5 represent the new configuration of solutions which can be expected. The range of choices GNM is reduced to the smaller area G^*N^*M. However, within these limits the prisoner's dilemma problem persists. Budgetary monitoring of the kind described here cannot bring about a situation in which the area GNM reduces to a single point (usually designated as the core) and thereby enable the organization to attain a cooperative group equilibrium.

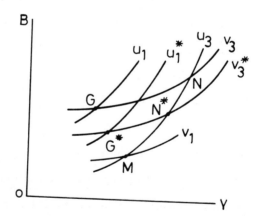

Figure 9.5. Monitoring the Group

One further observation is in order. When the budgetary monitoring is imposed on the workers they may

(a) decide to create changes in the quality of products which are not necessarily specified by the management, or

(b) produce some other related goods or create organizational investments which will improve their chances of resource diversions in the long run. This reduces the efficacy of budgetary control.

One of the sources of increased cost is the on-the-job leisure chosen by the worker's group. Hence, this can be related to the number of hours of work put in by the members in group G. They can be monitored somewhat more rigorously by asking them to record in and out time. It is evident that this approach has its limitations.

In more general terms, the budgetary allocations and audit procedures can extend to specific resource use. Such specific responsibility imposed on the group can at best reduce the limit on cash diversions to βM, $0 < \beta < 1$. It cannot guarantee that there will be a reduction in either costs of production or resource diversions. Further, there is a possibility that an equivalent budget reduction under overall value responsibility may be more acceptable to the worker's group so that conflicts can be minimized. This aspect of the problem, along with the excessive monitoring costs of specific responsibility, generally makes it a less desirable instrument of control.

On the whole, it can be concluded that monitoring the budgets and on-the-job leisure may reduce the opportunistic moves of the worker and enable the management to move toward a more desirable solution from their viewpoint. However, this is an incomplete approach to the problem and prisoner's dilemma like situations are more likely to persist.

Only one aspect of the information asymmetry has been considered in this section so far. It should also be recalled that production workers are farther away from the markets in which the management converts output into profits. Consequently, the worker's group experiences an information loss with respect to market price. The management may then appropriate a larger share of profits for itself and/or even keep the marginal value payments to the workers low. The worker's group can, at least conceptually, make an attempt to monitor the market price. Let $p^*(Y)$ be the estimated or expected price per unit of output Y which they produce. From this, given the budget B at which they are expected to produce Y, they have a perception of the relative gains accruing to them and the management. Depending on their attitudes toward the sharing of gains they can revise their estimate of market price and accordingly alter the budget negotiations with the manager. Stated in terms of the notions of Fig.9.5, such monitoring has the following effects:

(a) the lowest level of welfare which the group will accept increases to v_1^*,

(b) the group can restrict the management to u_3^* as their highest level of welfare. Consequently, the range of negotiated settlements can be reduced from GNM in Fig.9.6 to the area GN^*M^*. However, as with the management's monitoring of the workers, this approach of the group to elicit information about market prices may reduce the leverage of the management but cannot eliminate the persistence of prisoner's dilemma like situations. There will also be a tendency on the part of the management to creating product diversification, exploring new markets and such other strategies which will inhibit the monitoring process of the workers.

Monitoring by either one or both of the groups in the organizational interaction process may reduce the degree of exploitation of the other originating from the information impactedness which is experienced initially. However, these strategies are conflict prone, and mutually advantageous cooperative behavior cannot be assured. The management may use certain incentive mechanisms in an attempt to entice the workers towards a cooperative solution. These will be considered presently.

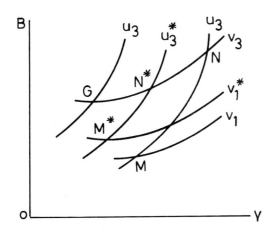

Figure 9.6. Market Information with the Group

9.6. INCENTIVES AND ORGANIZATIONAL BEHAVIOR

The alternative of providing incentives to the group, in an attempt to make them reveal the actual production domain, is available to the management. Though the incentive mechanisms can take on various forms, two major options will be considered in this section:

(a) an incentive to reduce cost by offering a part of the cost reduction achieved as a bonus, and

(b) profit sharing mechanisms.

Consider Fig.9.7. Under the assumptions of information asymmetry M^* is the total increase in budget over the minimum cost of production (C_g) which the worker's group can utilize to maximize their welfare. They attain a level v_e of welfare by choosing the point E. Suppose the management offers the group an incentive, of increasing payments to them by an amount αX; $0 < \alpha < 1$, to reduce their budget by X units. This means that the original estimate C_m, indicating the group's estimate of the management's information regarding the production domain, is too high.

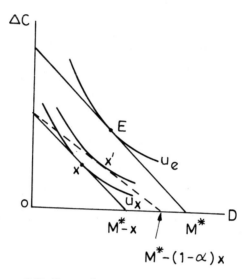

Figure 9.7. Incentives and Resource Diversions

Similarly, the management would have guessed that cost reduction is possible if they are offering an incentive to reduce costs. Under these conditions the group begins to realize that if they refuse to cooperate, the management can impose stricter control and reduce the budget to $M^* - X$. v_x will be the level of welfare possible under such conditions. If they accept the incentive then the constraint changes in such a way as to make them attain a welfare level $v_x^1 > v_x$ at the point x^1. Hence, the workers group will be better off if they accept the incentive and cooperate.

Suppose the incentive offered for reducing cost by X is in terms of a share of profits of the enterprise. This may be necessary to convince the workers that the results of their effort are not disproportionately appropriated by the management. The constraint for the group's decision may then cross M^* on the horizontal axis[82]. It can now be expected that a new level of welfare $v_i > v_e$ can be attained. Obviously, the total receipts of the group contain both resource diversions and the incentive payments. There is a possibility that profit sharing incentives reduce costs as well as resource diversions.

It should be obvious that such incentives can have the effect of eliciting greater cooperation even under specific responsibility. But, in general, the information asymmetry which the manager experiences would be such that the workers would be more inclined to cooperate when the profit sharing incentives are combined with overall value responsibility.

Both the group of workers as well as the managers may now feel that higher levels of v_3^* and u_3^* of welfare can be attained. Consequently, this increases the range of negotiation alternatives to $G^*N^*M^*$ as represented in Fig.9.8. However, neither the information asymmetry nor the differences in the objectives of the two decision makers have been altered. The persistence of mistrust and moral hazard may increase the area of conflict rather than move them toward greater cooperation[83]. There is no guarantee that the prisoner's dilemma situations will not persist.

9.7. CONCLUSION

Strategic choices available to the management cannot be fully described in terms of a few generic types. For example for the problems

---

[82] If the constraint does not cross over as indicated, the group cannot be made better off. They will not accept the incentives offered to them.

[83] Total agreement between the workers and the management regarding organizational goals and the decision making processes to achieve them may be necessary to obtain any durable solution. Indirect mechanisms, monitoring or incentives, cannot bring about a cooperative climate as desired. The worker's perception of equity in organizational decisions may be more important when labor management concepts are considered.

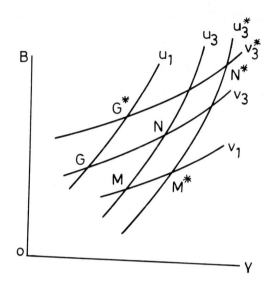

Figure 9.8. Incentives and Welfare

considered in this chapter, the management may consider the organizational structure giving rise to the information asymmetry in the first instance. Recall that in a divisionalized organization the group knows the production function. This is the source of their advantage and the observed increase in cost. But suppose each product department is further subdivisionalized on functional lines. Then the worker's group does not know the overall production domain. They may not be able to cheat as much now that they have only partial information regarding the production function. That is, a finely defined suborganization, essentially along functional lines within a divisionalized firm, may be capable of enabling the management to approximate the overall organizational goals more closely. In other words, matrix organizations may give certain strategic advantages to management. However, depending upon the perceptions and attitudes of the worker's group this may be a route to greater conflict rather than cooperation. The basic problems associated with the prisoner's dilemma situations persist.

Cooperative attitude and/or effective resolution of conflict in the organizational context does not develop unless there is a basic trust in each other's behavior. No amount of monitoring, penalties or incentives can assure increased efficiency. Such control mechanisms may temporarily create a semblence of cooperation but in the long run they will increase tensions and conflict. Negotiated and enduring equity in organizational decisions is far more important in obtaining a higher level of organizational performance. Organizational justice theories have an important bearing in such a milieu[84]. However, such stability and harmony in organizational functioning need not be conducive to growth. Even this line of argument suggests that enduring transitions from one disequilibrium state to another, along a desirable growth path would necessitate equity in decision making as a prerequisite for organizational consonance.

---

[84] For a review of details on this aspect see Greenberg (1987).

CHAPTER 10

IN RETROSPECT

10.1. TECHNICAL INEFFICIENCY REVISITED

The concept of technical efficiency is very well entrenched in the literature of welfare economics. However, much of the time it is defined in terms of the production function. In the standard neoclassical literature the production isoquants are assumed to be a well defined function

$$Y = f(x_1, x_2)$$

of the inputs. As such, for a given Y, there are a variety of combinations of (x_1, x_2) along the isoquant which represent the minimal inputs required in the production process. Every point along the isoquant is therefore considered to be technically efficient.

Technical inefficiency concepts and measurement usually proceed in the following manner. Referring to Fig.10.1, let p_1, p_2 be the prices of the factors of production and let E be the cost minimizing choice of inputs. If A is the actual choice of inputs made by the management draw a ray through A and the origin. If it intersects the isoquant at the point B then the ratio of inputs AB/OB can be considered as technical inefficiency. Equivalently, let C_a and C_b represent the isocost lines through the points A and B respectively. Then $C_a - C_b$ is taken to be the measure of technical inefficiency. It is obvious from the diagram that it can be measured equivalently by the quantity PQ where P and Q are on a ray through the point B and intersecting the isocost curves C_a and C_b respectively.

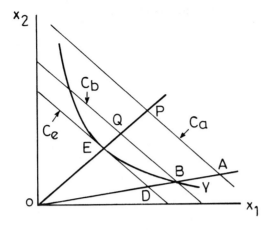

Figure 10.1. Technical Inefficiency

Notice that the ratio of the physical inputs is used as a measure of technical inefficiency only in the early work of Farrel (1957) and others. In most of the subsequent literature the cost interpretation has been preferred for obvious reasons of convenience in measurement. Further, as noted in Chapter 2, economic efficiency concepts are almost invariably expressed in terms of the costs of production. The question then is whether the cost functions can be directly utilized to estimate technical inefficiency. This has been a difficult proposition from a conceptual viewpoint. For, consider Fig.10.2. Assuming the factor prices to be given let LAC be the long run average cost curve and $AC(x_1)$ be a short run average cost curve such that the choice of x_1 is technically as well as economically efficient for an output Y_1. Suppose the firm is actually producing output Y_2 at the point A along the average cost curve AC_a. Given x_1, the technically efficient choice of inputs for the output Y_2 can be represented by the point T. Consequently the difference AT in the average cost represents technical inefficiency. Though this is conceptually as elegant as Fig.10.1

the measurement problems have been difficult.

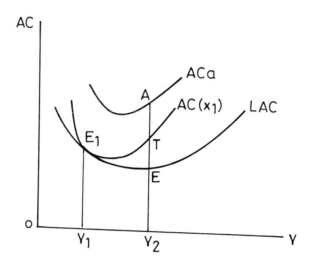

Figure 10.2. Technical Inefficiency and Costs

From the viewpoint of economic theory the more difficult question has always been the identification of the sources of technical inefficiency. Leibenstein's theory that the workers' motivations are a basic source have been shown to have its limitations. On the basis of the thesis of the present monograph it has been argued that certain managerial preferences can give rise to such inefficiencies. In particular, the generic specification of the lack of internal pressure explains technical inefficiency. Two questions are open for further analytical investigation:

(a) What are the sources of the managerial motivations represented by a particular specification of the lack of internal pressure?, and

(b) How are these motivations different from those which cause economic inefficiency?

In fact, it should be kept in perspective that even the conceptualization through Figs.10.1 and 10.2 implies that the factors responsible for technical inefficiency also generate economic inefficiency. To be sure, there can be other factors, related to the market for the output Y, which explain the emergence of economic inefficiency. As of now it is not clear if those influences can also generate technical inefficiency. The identification of these separate influences has certainly been a formidable task.

In realistic organizational situations the production functions themselves are not well defined. The very basis for defining technical inefficiency becomes nebulous even if the cost approach of Fig.10.2 is adopted. For, it is no longer obvious that the LAC and SAC concepts are well defined. The best that could be done is to show that the lack of internal pressure can still be considered as a source of inefficiency if the requisite cost functions are well defined.

The other problem in the literature arises in the context of vertically integrated firms. In a general sense, there are a variety of organizational choices which cannot be evaluated on the basis of a market price. Referring to the Coase diagram, Fig.3.1 of Chapter 3, it is clear that the inefficiency concepts can be defined if the average costs under the alternative organizational mode are known. Similarly, the lack of internal pressure will be a source of technical inefficiency if the alternative cost structures are known. But it is difficult to assert that such information is available.

The criticism that internal pressure as a source of technical inefficiency is an empty concept will remain until

(a) further analytical results can be developed to relate managerial motivations to specific preference functions, and

(b) estimation techniques can be developed to measure the degree of technical inefficiency in complex organizations.

10.2. ECONOMIC INEFFICIENCY REVISITED

Market demand concepts and consumer preferences are at the apex of the concepts of economic inefficiency. Much of the literature on welfare economics is devoted to examining various aspects of market imperfection as sources of economic inefficiency. In particular, the elasticity of demand, the number of firms, and barriers to entry have been cited.

As it turns out a definition of inefficiency based on costs alone is no longer considered to be adequate. Instead, it is expressed in terms of

(a) welfare to society,

(b) consumer surplus, or

(c) producer surplus.

These definitions have been controversial in so far as the distributional considerations are in conflict with the maximization of overall social welfare. Consider Fig.10.3. Let the choice of inputs be technically efficient

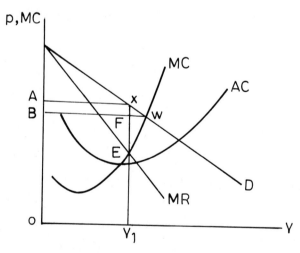

Figure 10.3. Economic Inefficiency

and AC and MC represent the average and marginal costs on this assumption. Then while W represents the welfare maximum the profit maximizing firm chooses an output Y_1. In the traditional literature on welfare economics the area XEW is defined as the loss in social welfare and is often designated as the dead weight loss or allocative inefficiency. However, it should be noted that the producer did not lose anything. On the contrary, there is a gain in terms of producer surplus or profit. That is, the entire welfare loss is incident on the consumers. It may be worthwhile to measure economic inefficiency in terms of the reduction in the consumer surplus.

Suppose there is a lack of internal pressure on the part of the management. That is, they are willing to accept a reduction in the level of profits in their pursuit of other objectives. In such a context the reduction in the observed profits is not a welfare loss. Redefining welfare loss in terms of the reduction in consumer surplus appears to be durable. However, Gravelle (1982), Utton (1982, pp. 61-62) and others are not willing to accept this on the premise that there is no justification for such a distributional weighting of the preferences of the different groups involved.

If the position is taken that managerial preferences being what they are social welfare definitions should accept them as such then it turns out that the only source of economic inefficiency is the nature of the market. Allocative inefficiency is the only relevant concept. On the other hand, if the consumers can be said to have a right to complain about their loss even when they are not in a position to influence managerial practices and/or public policy then there is a welfare loss over and above allocative inefficiency. In the present study this was designated as managerial inefficiency.

To begin with it should be reiterated that managerial inefficiency can arise even if there is no technical or allocative inefficiency. Secondly, it is obvious that managerial motivations can induce technical as well as economic inefficiency. The concept of the lack of internal pressure is useful even in such a context. Managerial motivations toward supplanting price competition by resorting to nonprice decisions can be examined within such a perspective. Even organizational decisions belong to this generic specification.

In the context of economic efficiency the more fundamental difficulty is in the welfare appraisal of nonprice decisions as they influence the market demand for the products of any one firm. This is as yet an unchartered area and is therefore subject to controversy.

Consider the observed or actual demand curve for the products of any one firm in monopolistic competition. Generally it is a result of three factors:

(a) consumer preferences,

(b) reactions of the consumers to nonprice strategies of the firm, and

(c) the choices of rival firms.

One of the fundamental problems has been the characterization of the consumer valuation of product differentiation and nonprice strategies of firms. It is generally accepted that when confronted with two differentiated products (or varieties of a product) the consumer can and does express a preference for one over the others. Thus, though the choice of product variety is a decision of the management of a firm the consumers can signal their valuation through the market.

However, product differentiation need not be only along the lines of product variety. It can represent variations in quality, advertising by the firm, packaging and presentation, as well as other characteristics like reliability of supply whenever the demand for the product is recurrent. In the literature on monopolistic competition it is assumed that the firm makes these choices and the consumer simply accepts them. For instance, post advertising demand curves have been adopted as a standard for welfare measurement. However, suppose that two firms differ in their levels of advertising or their inventory. Is it possible that consumer preference for the product of one of these firms over the other is influenced by such non-price decisions? It appears that the answer is in the affirmative. That is, the demand curve for a firm, as it manifests itself on the market, contains an implicit valuation of certain nonprice decisions.

It is of course clear that certain nonprice decisions of a firm, such as the purely organizational aspects which influence the cost, do not enter the consumer valuation. They either do not have any effect on the reliability of supply or the price charged or the consumers cannot value such influences. The problem is one of ascertaining whether a particular nonprice decision does or does not enter the consumer valuation of the product. As a rule of thumb it may be suggested that whenever the consumers can infer that a nonprice decision, such as quality or advertising has the effect on the price of the product they will have an implicit valuation for the nonprice decisions of the firm. Only in those situations where the nonprice decisions have an exclusive effect on the cost of production will it be difficult to have a consumer valuation.

In essence, from the viewpoint of welfare analysis, consumer valuation of nonprice decisions must be explicitly taken into account while defining economic inefficiency. When this is done there is an inefficiency in the choice of the nonprice dimension which in turn manifests itself in the form of an inefficient choice in the level of output. One of the sources of this kind of inefficiency is of course the lack of internal pressure.

The problems of economic inefficiency are compounded if the management can succeed in creating certain barriers to entry in the operation of the market mechanism. One of the manifestations of economic power created due to barriers to entry is of course the shift to the right of the demand curve indicated by the preferences of the consumers. To evolve a generic concept this has been designated as the lack of external pressure.

The practical difficulty in the implementation of such a concept is the identification of the ceiling demand curve which embodies consumer valuation of nonprice decisions. The identification of the concept itself appears to be important in facilitating measurement. This is the spirit in which the analysis of quality of products and advertising was taken up.

10.3. OTHER CONCEPTUAL PROBLEMS

The entire set of problems associated with managerial inefficiency can be said to originate in the existence of organizational slack. In monopolistic short run equilibrium this takes the form of a positive profit. In a vertically integrated firm the cost advantage relative to the market price of inputs explains the discretionary surplus. If the surplus is actually generated and distributed to the various groups in exchange in turn economic analysis generally gives an approval and posits that efficient choices are made. On the other hand, if the surplus is even partially utilized to reallocate resources the cost increases are recorded and managerial inefficiency is said to have emerged. To some observers this appears to be purely a consequence of the cost accounting conventions.

In complex hierarchical organizations there is necessarily a certain amount of delegation of authority with respect to resource utilization. Under these conditions none of the decision makers would be able to assess the impact on the overall costs of their own decisions. At best each of them can make an effort to minimize the costs attribtuable to their specific department or division. This can give rise to overall cost minimization if and only if the transfer price mechanisms are efficient. This rarely happens in practice.

On the whole the relevant cost concepts for welfare analysis are yet to be concretely developed. The ambiguity in the notion of minimum cost at which a given output can be produced persists unless an incentive compatible organizational mechanism can be identified.

Certain organizational decisions of the nonprice nature have been shown to increase welfare even if the maximum possible is not attained. However, in some complex organizations it is difficult to ascertain the degree to which each of the managerial teams and their decisions contribute to overall welfare. The role of maximum welfare as an economic efficiency concept needs reconsideration.

In a similar fashion the definition of the overall welfare level is contingent on the autonomy of each of the decision makers in their choice and the relative weights assigned to them. Naturally the economic inefficiency concepts are controversial unless one common definition of social welfare is accepted. Attempts in this direction have been generally frustrating.

Even when a set of concepts of economic welfare and sources of inefficiency have been identified there have been difficulties in

(a) estimating unobservable preference functions of consumers for certain nonprice decisions as well as managerial preference functions, and

(b) delimiting the sources and the extent of technological, economic, and managerial inefficiencies.

A single omnibus definition of economic efficiency has not been adequate for identifying the efficiency of nonprice and organizational decisions.

Stated somewhat differently the neoclassical convention of the difference between the price of a unit of output and the marginal cost being the contribution of social welfare is becoming untenable. The primary reason for this is that it is not sustainable in practice in hierarchical organizations with delegation of power.

Despite the progress made in defining social costs following Coase (1960) the problem of cost in any practical organizational setting remains elusive. The progress made in this study can be consolidated only by iteratively examining the conceptual and empirical implications. Movement toward efficient nonprice and organizaional decisions can only be incremental and iterative.

BIBLIOGRAPHY

1. Ackerman, S.R., The Economics of Nonprofit Institutions (New York: Oxford University Press, 1986).

2. Aiginger, K., The Impact of Risk Attitude, Uncertainty and Disequilibrium on Optimal Production and Inventroy, Theory and Decision, 1985, pp. 51-75.

3. Alchian, A.A., Costs and Outputs, in P.A. Baran (ed.), The Allocation of Economic Resources (Stanford: Stanford University Press, 1959).

4. Alchian, A.A., and H. Demsetz, Production, Information Costs, and Economic Organization, American Economic Review, December 1972, pp. 777-795.

5. Alessi, L.D., Property Rights, Transaction Costs, and X-Efficiency : An Essay in Economic Theory, American Economic Review, March 1983, pp. 64-81.

6. Amey, L.R., The Efficiency of Business Enterprises (London: Allen and Unwin, 1969).

7. Arvan,L., Dynamic Monopoly Production, Inventory, and Price Policy Under Sophisticated Demand, Economics Letters, 1982, pp. 191-194.

8. Arvan, L., and L.N. Moses, Inventory Investment and the Theory of the Firm, American Economic Review, March 1982, pp. 186-193.

9. Bates, J., and J.R. Parkinson, Business Economics (Oxford: Basil Blackwell, 1982).

10. Bailey, E.E., and A.F. Friedlander, Market Structure and Multiproduct Industries, Journal of Economic Literature, September 1982, pp. 1024-1048.

11. Baumol, W.J., Business Behavior, Value and Growth (New York: Macmillan, 1959).

12. Baumol, W.J., et al., Contestable Markets and the Theory of Industry Structure (New York: Harcourt, 1982).

13. Beckmann, M.J., Management Production Functions and Economic Theory, Journal of Economic Theory, 1977, pp. 1-18.

14. Beckmann, M.J., Tinbergen Lectures on Organization Theory (New York: Springer-Verlag, 1983).

15. Berle, A.A., and G.C. Means, The Modern Corporation and Private Property (New York: Harcourt, 1968).

16. Blinder, A.S., Inventories and Sticky Prices: More on the Micro-foundations of Macroeconomics, American Economic Review, June 1982, pp. 334-348.

17. Blinder, A.S., Can the Production Smoothing Model of Inventory Behavior by Saved?, Quarterly Journal of Economics, August 1986, pp. 431-454.

18. Burton, R.M., and B. Obel, Designing Efficient Organizations: Modelling and Experimentation (Amsterdam: North Holland, 1984).

19. Butters, G.R., Equilibrium Distributions of Sales and Advertising Prices, Review of Economic Studies, October 1977, pp. 465-492.

20. Calvo, G.A., and F.E. Thoumi, Demand Fluctuations, Inventories and Capacity Utilization, Southern Economic Journal, January 1984, pp. 743-754.

21. Calvo, G.A., and S. Wellisz, Supervision, Loss of Control and the Optimum Size of the Firm, Journal of Political Economy, October 1978, pp. 948-952.

22. Carlton, D.W., Vertical Integration in Competitive Markets Under Uncertainty, Journal of Industrial Economics, March 1979, pp. 189-209.

23. Caves, R.E., Corporate Strategy and Structure, Journal of Economic Literature, March 1980, pp. 64-92.

24. Chamberlin, E.H., The Theory of Monopolistic Competition (Cambridge: Harvard University Press, 1962).

25. Chandler, A.D., Strategy and Structure (Cambridge: M.I.T. Press, 1962).

26. Chandler, A.D., The Visible Hand: The Managerial Revolution in American Business (Cambridge: Harvard, 1977).

27. Cheung, S.N.S., The Contractual Nature of the Firm, Journal of Law and Economics, April 1983, pp. 1-21.

28. Chikan, A., Economics and Management of Inventories (Amsterdam: North Holland, 1981).

29. Chikan, A., Inventory in Theory and Practice (Amsterdam: Elsevier, 1986).

30. Clemens, E.W., Price Discrimination and the Multiproduct Firm, Review of Economic Studies, 1951, pp. 1-11.

31. Coase, R.H., The Nature of the Firm, Economica, November 1937, pp. 386-405.

32. Coase, R.H., Monopoly Pricing with Interrelated Costs and Demands, Economica, November 1946, pp. 278-294.

33. Coase, R.H., The Distinction Between Private and Social Benefits and Costs, Journal of Law and Economics, October 1960, pp. 1-44.

34. Comanor, W.S., and T.A. Wilson, Advertising, Market Structure, and Economic Performance, Review of Economics and Statistics, November 1967, pp. 423-440.

35. Comanor, W.S., and H. Leibenstein, Allocative Efficiency, X-Efficiency and the Measurement of Welfare Loss, Economica, August 1969, pp. 304-309.

36. Currie, J.M., J.A. Murphy and A. Schmitz, The Concept of Economic Surplus and Its Use in Economic Analysis, Economic Journal, December 1971, pp. 741-799.

37. Cyert, R.M., and J.G. March, A Behavioral Theory of the Firm (Engelwood Cliffs: Prentice Hall, 1965).

38. Daughety, A.F., Stochastic Production and Cost, Southern Economic Journal, July 1982, pp. 106-118.

39. Dean, J., Statistical Cost Estimation (Bloomington: Indiana University Press, 1976).

40. Dixit, A.K., and V. Norman, Advertising and Welfare, Bell Journal of Economics, Spring 1978, pp. 1-17.

41. Dobb, M., Welfare Economics and the Economics of Socialism (Cambridge: Cambridge University Press, 1969).

42. Dreze, J.H., and K.P. Hagen, Choice of Product Quality: Equilibrium and Efficiency, Econometrica, May 1978, pp. 493-514.

43. Fama, E.F., Agency Problems and the Theory of the Firm, Journal of Political Economy, April 1980, pp. 288-307.

44. Fershtman, C., Learning by Doing, Inventory and Optimal Price Policy, Journal of Economics and Business, February 1986, pp. 19-26.

45. FitzRoy, F.R., and D.C. Muller, Cooperation and Conflict in Contractual Organizations, Quarterly Review of Economics and Business, Winter 1984, pp. 24-49.

46. Francis, A., Company Objectives, Managerial Motivations and the Behavior of Large Firms, Cambridge Journal of Economics, 1980, pp. 349-361.

47. Glick, R., and C. Whilborg, Price and Output Adjustment, Inventory Flexibility, and Cost and Demand Disturbances, Canadian Journal of Economics, August 1985, pp. 566-573.

48. Gold, B., New Perspectives on Cost Theory and Empirical Findings, Journal of Industrial Economics, April 1966, pp. 164-197.

49. Gold, B., Changing Perspectives on Size, Scale, and Returns: An Interpretive Survey, Journal of Economic Literature, March 1981, pp. 5-33.

50. Gravelle, H.S.E., Incentives, Efficiency and Control in Public Firms, Zeitschrift fur Nationalokonomie, Supplement 1982, pp. 79-104.

51. Gravelle, H.S.E., and R. Rees, Microeconomics (London: Longmans, 1981).

52. Greenberg, J., Taxonomy of Organizational Justice Theories, Academy of Management Review, January 1987, pp. 9-22.

53. Grossman, G.M., and C. Shapiro, Informative Advertising with Differentiated Products, Review of Economic Studies, January 1984, pp. 63-81.

54. Hage, J., Theories of Organizations (New York: Wiley, 1980).

55. Harris, S., C.H. Kriebel, and A. Raviv, Asymmetric Information, Incentives, and Intrafirm Resource Allocation, Management Science, June 1982, pp. 604-620.

56. Hart, O.D., Monopolistic Competition in the Spirit of Chamberlin: Special Results, Economic Journal, December 1985, pp. 889-908.

57. Hay, D.A., and D.J. Morris, Industrial Economics (Oxford: Oxford University Press, 1979).

58. Heiner, R.A., Imperfect Decisions in Organizations, Journal of Economic Behavior and Organization, January 1988, pp. 25-44.

59. Hess, J.D., The Economics of Organization (Amsterdam: North Holland, 1983).

60. Hicks, J.R., Annual Survey of Economic Theory: The Theory of Monopoly, Econometrica, 1935, pp. 1-20.

61. Hill, C.W.L., Organizational Structure, the Development of the Firm and Business Behavior, in J.F. Pickering and T.A.J. Cokerill (eds.) The Economic Management of the Firm (New Delhi: Heritage, 1984).

62. Hirschleifer, J., Economics of the Divisionalized Firm, Journal of Business, April 1957, pp. 96-108.

63. Hirschleifer, J., and J.G. Riley, The Analytics of Uncertainty and Information: An Expository Survey, Journal of Economic Literature, December 1979, pp. 1375-1421.

64. Hoenack, S.A., Economic Behavior Within Organizations (New York: Cambridge University Press, 1983).

65. Hubbard, L.J., Ex Ante and Ex Post Long-Run Average Cost Functions, Applied Economics, 1987, pp. 1411-1419.

66. Ireland, N.J., and P.J. Law, The Economics of Labor-Managed Enterprises (London: Croom Helm, 1982).

67. Irish, M.J., Optimal Quality Choice: An Empirical Study, Oxford Bulletin of Economics and Statistics, May 1980, pp. 65-78.

68. Jensen, M.C., and W.H. Meckling, Thoery of the Firm: Managerial Behavior, Agency Costs and Ownership Structure, Journal of Financial Economics, October 1976, pp. 305-360.

69. Jones, G.R., and J.E. Butler, Costs, Revenue, and Business Level Strategy, Academy of Management Review, April 1988, pp. 202-213.

70. Kahn, A.E., The Economics of Regulation (New York: Wiley, 1971).

71. Kahn, J.A., Inventories and the Volatility of Production, American Economic Review, September 1987, pp. 667-679.

72. Keren, M., and D. Levhari, The Optimum Span of Control in a Pure Hierarchy, Management Science, September 1979, pp. 1162-1172.

73. Keren, M., and D. Levhari, The Internal Organization of the Firm and the Shape of the Average Costs, Bell Journal of Economics, 1983, pp. 474-486.

74. Klein, B., R.G. Crawford and A.A. Alchian, Vertical Integration, Appropriable Rents, and Competitive Contracting Process, Journal of Law and Economics, October 1978, pp. 297-326.

75. Klein, B., and K.B. Leffler, The Role of Market Forces in Assuring Contractual Performance, Journal of Political Economy, August 1981, pp. 615-641.

76. Knetch, J.L., and J.A. Sinden, Willingness to Pay and Compensation Demanded: Experimental Evidence of an Unexpected Disparity in Measures of Value, Quarterly Journal of Economics, December 1984, pp. 507-521.

77. Knight, F.H., The Economic Organization (New York: Harper, 1951).

78. Knight, F.H., Risk, Uncertainty and Profit (New York: Harper, 1965).

79. Kono, T., Strategy and Structure of Japanese Enterprises (London: Macmillan, 1984).

80. Kotowitz, Y., and F. Mathewson, Advertising, Consumer Information, and Product Quality, Bell Journal of Economics, Autumn 1979, pp. 566-588.

81. Lambin, J.J., Advertising, Competition and Market Conduct in Oligopoly Over Time (Amsterdam: North Holland, 1976).

82. Langlois, R.N., Internal Organization in a Dynamic Context: Some Theoretical Considerations, in M. Jussawala and H. Ebenfield (eds.) Communication and Information Economics (Amsterdam: Elsevier, 1984).

83. Leibenstein, H., Economic Theory and Organizational Analysis (New York: Harper, 1960).

84. Leibenstein, H., Allocative vs X-Efficiency, American Economic Review, June 1966, pp. 392-415.

85. Leibenstein, H., Beyond Economic Man (Cambridge: Harvard, 1980).

86. Leibenstein, H., and W.S. Comanor, Allocative Efficiency, X-Efficiency and the Measurement of Welfare Loss, Economica, August 1969, pp. 304-309.

87. Leland, H.E., Quality Choice and Competition, American Economic Review, March 1977, pp. 127-135.

88. Levhari, D., and T.N. Srinivasan, Durability of Consumption Goods: Competition vs. Monopoly, American Economic Review, March 1969, pp. 102-107.

89. Loon, P.V., A Dynamic Theory of the Firm: Production, Finance and Investment (Berlin: Springer Verlag, 1983).

90. Macdonald, G.M., Information and Production, Econometrica, September 1982, pp. 1143-1162.

91. Macdonald, G.M., New Directions in the Theory of Agency, Canadian Journal of Economics, August 1984, pp. 415-440.

92. Malcolmson, J.M., Work Incentives, Hierarchy, and Internal Labor Markets, Journal of Political Economy, June 1984, pp. 486-507.

93. Malmgren, H.B., Information, Expectations and the Theory of the Firm, Quarterly Journal of Economics, August 1961, pp. 399-421.

94. March, J.G., and H.A. Simon, Organizations (New York: Wiley, 1963).

95. Marris, R., The Economic Theory of Managerial Capitalism (London: Macmillan, 1964).

96. Marris, R., and D.C. Muller, The Corporation, Competition and the Invisible Hand, Journal of Economic Literature, March 1980, pp. 32-63.

97. Marris, R., and A. Wood, The Corporate Economy (London: Macmillan, 1971).

98. Marschak, J., Efficient and Viable Organizational Forms, in M. Haire (ed.) Modern Organizational Research (New York: Wiley, 1954).

99. Marshall, J.D., et al., Agent's Evaluations and Disparity in Measures of Economic Loss, Journal of Economic Behavior and Organization, June 1986, pp. 115-128.

100. McFadden, D., Cost, Revenue, and Profit Functions in M. Fuss and D. McFadden (eds.) Production Function Economics: A Dual Approach to Theory and Applications (Amsterdam: North Holland, 1978).

101. Mcgee, J.S., and L.R. Bassett, Vertical Integration Revisited, Journal of Law and Economics, April 1976, pp. 17-38.

102. McKie, J.M., Organization and Efficiency, Southern Economic Journal, April 1972, pp. 449-458.

103. Miller, H.L., On the Theory of Demand for Consumer Durables, Southern Economic Journal, April 1961, pp. 1249-1252.

104. Mirrlees, J.A., The Optimum Structure of Incentives and Authority Within an Organization, Bell Journal of Economics, Spring 1976, pp. 105-131.

105. Mishan, J., Introduction to Normative Economics (New York: Oxford Unversity Press, 1981).

106. Moss, S., The History of the Theory of the Firm, Economica, August 1984, pp. 307-318.

107. Murphy, M.M., Price Controls and the Behavior of the Firm, International Economic Review, June 1980, pp. 285-292.

108. Nelson, P., Advertising and Information, Journal of Political Economy, July 1974, pp. 729-754.

109. Nichols, L.M., Advertising and Economic Welfare, American Economic Review, March 1985, pp. 213-218.

110. Odagiri, H., The Theory of Growth in a Corporate Economy (Cambridge: Cambridge University Press, 1981).

111. Oren, S., Pricing a Product Line, Journal of Business, January 1984, pp. 73-99.

112. Otani, H., The Price Determination in the Inventory Stock Market: A Disequilibrium Analysis, International Economic Review, October 1983, pp. 709-719.

113. Parks, R.W., The Demand and Supply of Durable Goods and Durability, American Economic Review, March 1974, pp. 37-54.

114. Penrose, E.T., The Theory of the Growth of the Firm (New York: Wiley, 1959).

115. Phillips, A., Market Structure, Organization, and Performance (Cambridge: Harvard University Press, 1962).

116. Phlips, L., The Economics of Price Discrimination (Cambridge: Cambridge University Press, 1983).

117. Pickering, J.F., and T.A.J. Cockerill, The Economic Management of the Firm (New Delhi: Heritage, 1984).

118. Pontryagin, L.S., et al., The Mathematical Theory of Optimal Processes (New York: Wiley, 1962).

119. Radner, R., A Behavioral Model of Cost Reduction, Bell Journal of Economics, Spring 1975, pp. 196-215.

120. Radner, R., The Internal Economy of Large Firms, Economic Journal, Conference Papers, 1986, pp. 1-22.

121. Reekie, W.D., Industry, Prices and Markets (New York: Wiley, 1979).

122. Scherer, F.M., Industrial Market Structure and Economic Performance (Chicago: Rand McNally, 1980).

123. Schutte, D.P., Optimal Inventories and Equilibrium Price Behavior, Journal of Economic Theory, June 1984, pp. 46-58.

124. Seshinski, E., Price, Quality, and Quantity Regulation in Monopoly Situation, Economica, May 1976, pp. 127-137.

125. Sharkey, W.W., The Theory of Natural Monopoly (Cambridge: Cambridge University Press, 1982).

126. Shilony, Y., Surplus May Measure Waste, Journal of Public Economics, December 1983, pp. 363-374.

127. Sieper, E., and P.L. Swan, Monopoly and Competition in the Market for Durable Goods, Reivew of Economic Studies, July 1973, pp. 333-352.

128. Silver, M., Enterprise and the Scope of the Firm: The Role of Vertical Integration (Oxford:Martin Robertson, 1984).

129. Simon, H.A., Models of Bounded Rationality, Vols. 1 and 2 (Cambridge: M.I.T. Press, 1982).

130. Spence, M., The Economics of Internal Organization: An Introduction, Bell Journal of Economics, Spring 1975, pp. 163-172.

131. Spence, M., Nonlinear Prices and Welfare, Journal of Public Economics, January 1977, pp. 1-18.

132. Spence, M., Nonprice Competition, American Economic Review, Febraury 1977, pp. 255-259.

133. Spulber, D.F., Risk Sharing and Inventories, Journal of Economic Behavior and Organization, March 1985, pp. 55-68.

134. Stigler, G.J., The Existence of X-Efficiency, American Economic Review, March 1976, pp. 213-216.

135. Stiglitz, J.E., Incentives, Risk and Information: Notes Toward a Theory of Hierarchy, Bell Journal of Economics, Autumn 1975, pp. 552-579.

136. Sweeny, J.L., Quality, Commodity Hierarchies, and the Housing Market, Econometrica, January 1974, pp. 147-167.

137. Teece, D.J., Economies of Scope and the Scope of the Enterprise, Journal of Economic Behavior and Organization, September 1980, pp. 223-247.

138. Teece, D.J. Towards a Theory of the Multiproduct Firm, Journal of Economic Behavior and Organization, March 1982, pp. 869-872.

139. Teece, D.J., Transaction Cost Economics and the Multi-National Enterprise: An Assessment, Journal of Economic Behavior and Organization, March 1986, pp. 21-46.

140. Utton, M.A., The Political Economy of Big Business (Oxford: Martin Robertson, 1982).

141. Vanek, J., The General Theory of Labor-Managed Economies (Ithaca: Cornell, 1970).

142. Ware, R., Inventory Holding as a Strategic Weapon to Deter Entry, Economica, February 1985, pp. 93-101.

143. Weckstein, R.S., Welfare Criteria and Changing Tastes, American Economic Review, March 1982, pp. 133-153.

144. Weizsacker, C.C., The Costs of Substitution, Econometrica, September 1984, pp. 1085-1116.

145. Whitin, T.M., Inventory Control and Price Theory, Management Science, October 1955.

146. Wiggins, S.N., and W.J. Lane, Quality Uncertainty, Search, and Advertising, American Economic Review, December 1983, pp. 881-894.

147. Williamson, O.E., The Economics of Discretionary Behavior: Managerial Objectives in a Theory of the Firm (Engelwood Cliffs: Prentice Hall, 1964).

148. Williamson, O.E., Hierarchical Control and the Optimum Firm Size, Journal of Political Economy, April 1967, pp. 123-138.

149. Williamson, O.E., Corporate Control and Business Behavior (Engelwood Cliffs: Prentice Hall, 1970).

150. Williamson, O.E., The Vertical Integration of Production: Market Failure Considerations, American Economic Review, May 1971, pp. 112-123.

151. Williamson, O.E., Markets and Heirarchies: Some Elementary Considerations, American Economic Review, May 1973, pp. 316-325.

152. Williamson, O.E., The Economics of Antitrust: Transaction Cost Considerations, University of Pennsylvania Law Review, 1974, pp. 1439-1496.

153. Williamson, O.E., The Economics of Internal Governance: Exit and Voice in Relation to Markets and Hierarchies, American Economic Review, May 1976, pp. 369-377.

154. Williamson, O.E., Transaction Cost Economics: The Governance of Contractual Relations, Journal of Law and Economics, October 1979, pp. 233-261.

155. Williamson, O.E., The Modern Corporation: Origins, Evolution, and Attributes, Journal of Economic Literature, December 1981, pp. 1537-1568.

156. Williamson, O.E., The Economics of Governance: Framework and Implications, Journal of Institutional and Theoretical Economics, March 1984, pp. 1085-1116.

157. Williamson, O.E., The Economic Institutions of Capitalism (New York: Free Press, 1985).

158. Williamson, O.E., and W.G. Ouchi, The Markets and Hierarchies Program of Research: Origins, Implications, and Progress, in A.H. Van der Ven and W.F. Joyce (eds.) Perspectives on Organizational Design and Behavior (New York: Wiley, 1981).

159. Wood, A., Economic Analysis of the Corporate Economy, in R. Marris and A. Wood (eds.) The Corporate Economy (London: Macmillan, 1971).

160. Wright, B.D., and J.C. Williams, The Welfare Effects of the Introduction of Storage, Quarterly Journal of Economics, February 1984, pp. 169-192.

INDEX

W. Gaul, M. Schader (Eds.)

Data, Expert Knowledge and Decisions

An Interdisciplinary Approach with Emphasis on Marketing Applications

1988. VIII, 380 pp. 117 figs. ISBN 3-540-19038-4

Cross-disciplinary research on how computer-assisted decision making can be supported by sophisticated data analysis techniques and recent developments in knowledge-based systems research are described in this volume, with emphasis on marketing applications.

G. Fandel, H. Dyckhoff, J. Reese (Eds.)

Essays on Production Theory and Planning

1988. XII, 223 pp. 48 figs., 46 tabs. ISBN 3-540-19314-6

The thirteen essays of this book deal with aspects of production management which have shown a growing importance in research, teaching and practice within the last few years.

G. Fandel (Ed.)

Management Problems in Health Care

1988. IX, 297 pp. 29 figs. 43 tabs. ISBN 3-540-19243-3

The treatment and solution of health economic problems by the use of management concepts is a permanent challenge. It is a question of controlling the costs or the efficiency of the supply of medical services. The articles in this book provide a significant contribution to this subject by reporting on the latest research the authors have done in this area.

Springer-Verlag Berlin Heidelberg New York London Paris Tokyo Hong Kong

Springer